Sensational Cakes

Sylvia Weinstock's

Sensational Cakes

Written with Donna Bulseco
Principal Photography by John Labbe
Book Design by Doug Turshen with David Huang

Stewart, Tabori & Chang
New York

Dedication & Acknowledgments

In my lifetime, I have been fortunate to meet and work with so many wonderful, smart, creative, and fun people, from the artists in my studio—the bakers, flower makers, designers, decorators, builders, and packers—to the wedding planners, florists, caterers, restaurateurs, and administrators out in the field. The business I am in is filled with people who inspire me. I want to thank them all for the immense pleasure and help they have given me throughout the years.

Of course, I want to dedicate this book to my husband, Ben, who is at the heart of everything I do. He has been my support and love of my life, helping, inspiring, and keeping me happily on track through it all.

Many thanks go to the team on this book, especially Doug Turshen and David Huang for the beautiful design, Donna Bulseco for capturing my thoughts and words, John Labbe for the exquisite photography, and my editors Jennifer Levesque and Leslie Stoker at Stewart, Tabori & Chang for their interest and support.

A Touch of Blue
Page 54

Utterly Feminine
Page 86

Just for the Fun of It
Page 162

The Art of Making a Cake
Page 194

Introduction

Create Some Magic

Let's have a party. That simple phrase is a call to action to let the excitement begin. When people throw a party, magic happens. In the close to 30 years I've been making cakes, I've seen many beautiful parties, and they come in all shapes and sizes. The best celebrate the moment in special ways: gorgeous flowers, delicious food and wines, creative décor, inspiring toasts, and, last but not least, a sensational cake. A cake is a quintessential part of the ritual. There's nothing like a party to recharge your batteries, and I've seen how something as simple as a cake can enchant guests and enhance their experience. A cake, it turns out, is more than just dessert—and serves many purposes at a party. It's decoration, a conversation starter, a backdrop for photos, and a keepsake. Sometimes it is the one concrete memory guests retain of the entire event—simply because it was beautiful and delicious.

What is the secret to creating a sensational cake? Inspiration and artistry are important, as is attention to detail. Work, work, and more work certainly comes into play, as well as the skill and artistry of a team of baking professionals. But what's at the core for me is the desire to make something truly beautiful. (I've often thought my own desire comes from the fact that I never had a wedding cake!) That's why I want those who come to me to have exactly what they want— and why I hope this book inspires you to create sensational cakes of your own. In my experience, people remember what they *didn't* get. (To this day, I think back to an apricot gabardine suit with a certain longing.) My feeling is, *go for it.* Later in life, you never want to say, "I should have . . . !"

My First Cake

People often ask how I got started. Looking back, I realize there's no way I could have predicted the course of my life. My parents were immigrants—hard workers who didn't have time for the niceties in life. In fact, my mother couldn't cook, and we didn't usually sit down to a dinner table set with linen napkins, candles, and properly placed cutlery. When I married, that's what I wanted. I was a young bride and didn't know the domestic three girls, and I became a homemaker. I learned to sew, knit, garden, cook, and entertain—and I found entertaining pleasurable. Making desserts was especially rewarding: a pot roast could be good, but the dessert table was what everyone remembered. I liked the accolades! As an amateur, I followed the rules, and recipes came out fine. But there were formulas I didn't understand, so my experiments often failed.

Luckily for me, I found wonderful teachers.

A cake is a quintessential part of a party ritual. As it turns out, a cake is more than just dessert: It's decoration, a conversation starter, a backdrop for photos, and sometimes even a keepsake.

arts, but I learned quickly. Of course, I got a cookbook—*Mastering the Art of French Cooking,* by Julia Child with Simone Beck—and I went through it torturous page by torturous page. I graduated to cookbooks by Maida Heatter and Dione Lucas, a great baker; I loved her chocolate soufflé rolls.

When I graduated from Hunter College, I became a schoolteacher; my husband went to New York University and became a lawyer. We moved to Long Island, and after about five years and a few dollars in the bank, we started a family. We had My daughters and husband were skiers, and we often went to an inn upstate that was frequented by a multitude of chefs. One of the retired pastry chefs took me on, and I excelled enough to start selling desserts to a local restaurant. William Greenberg, who was the proprietor of several New York City bakeries, told me there was no one who could do a beautiful cake that was delicious—inevitably it would have been baked days before because it took that long to decorate. Fondant, which is sugar clay you can't refrigerate once it's rolled out onto a

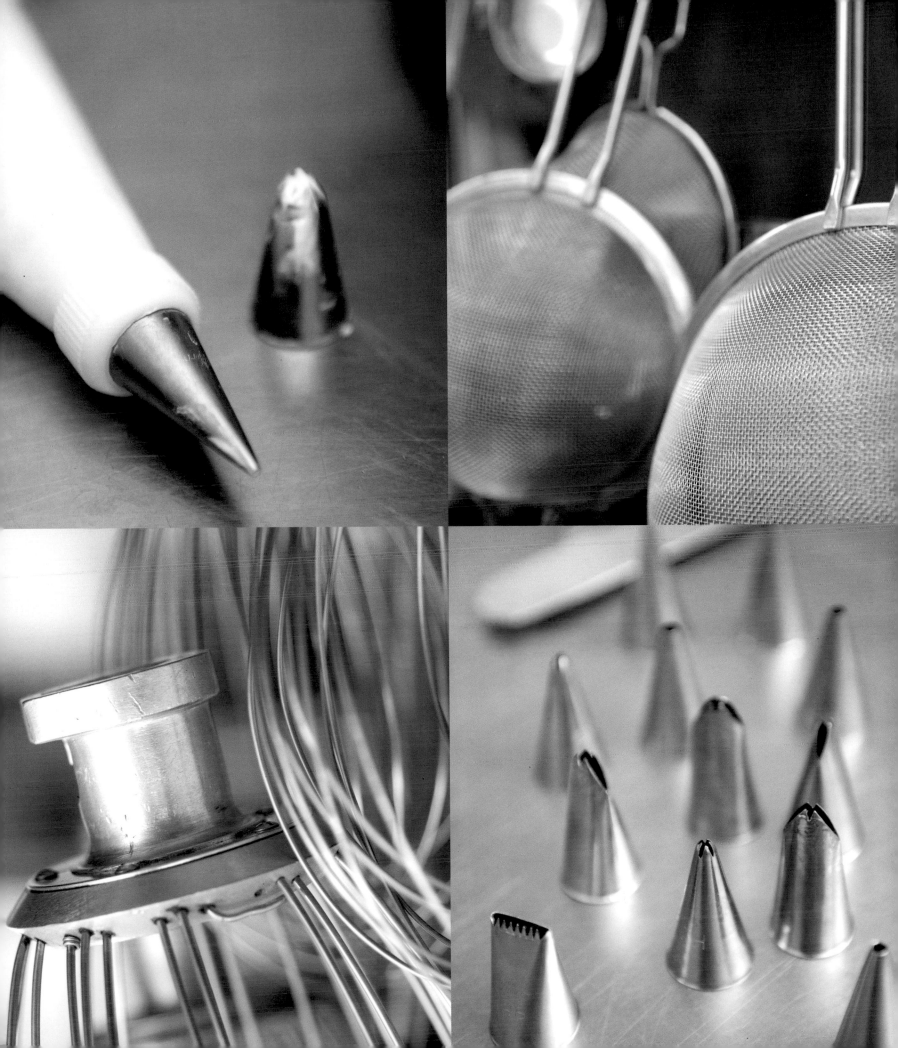

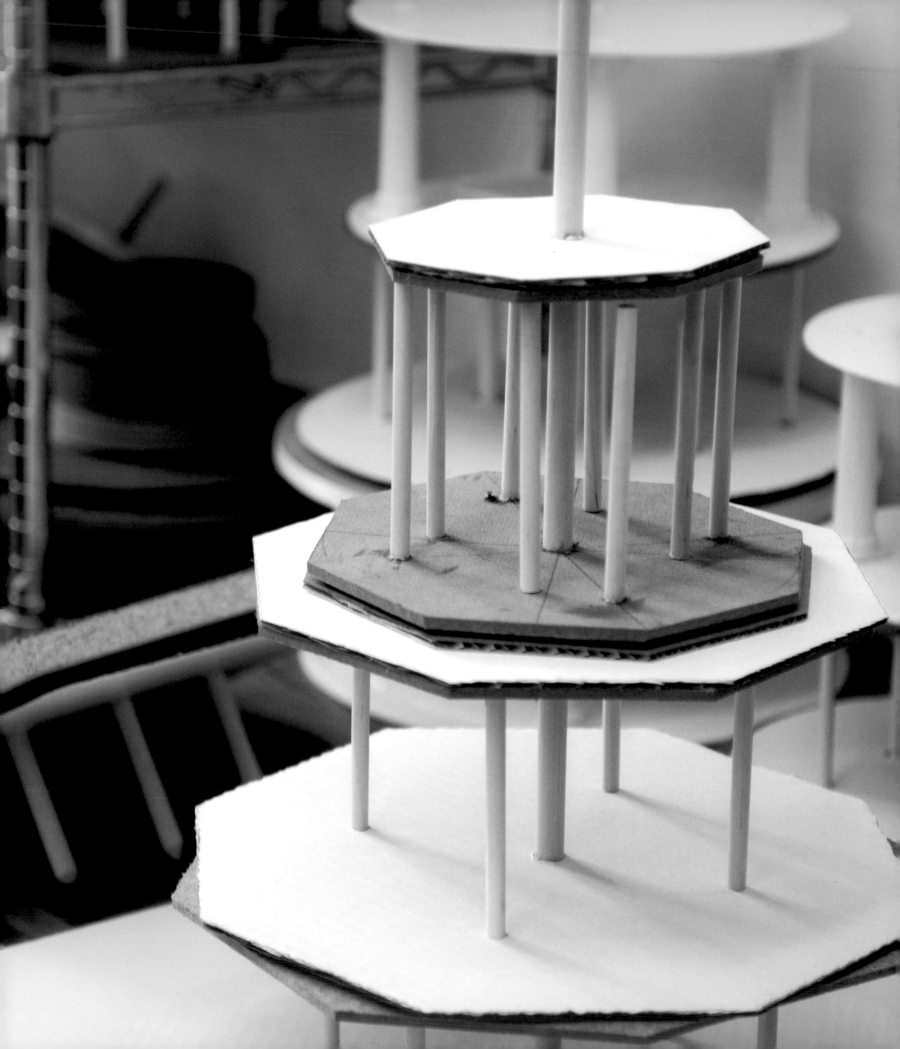

cake, was a big part of the problem. I hate fondant! Instead, I use buttercream—it's delicious, and easy to cut and serve.

My big breakthrough came when I sold a cake to a little shop in Chelsea. The owner thought the one-tiered cake filled with flowers was so gorgeous she put it in the window, and a chef who worked for Donald Bruce White, a big society

original brides, making cakes for engagements, showers, rehearsal dinners, and often grooms' cakes. Then come the wedding cakes, cakes for the first baby, the thirteenth birthday, or a Sweet Sixteen. We've done the off-to-college cake; then the children get engaged, and we start the process all over again. It's nice to be part of a life cycle—you're part of the family.

When it comes to the design, you should always have some idea of what you want. Bring photos of what appeals to you when you meet with your cake maker.

caterer, saw it. White started ordering my cakes for all his very special ladies. One of them ordered it for an event at the Carlyle Hotel, and all of a sudden my cakes were at parties at the Plaza, the Pierre, the Metropolitan Club, and big society weddings at St. Patrick's Cathedral.

Although we like to think our cakes make a wedding immortal, that's not always the case—we don't guarantee the marriage; we only guarantee the cake. It has been a privilege to bake cakes for some of this country's most well known people. I've been in New York City since 1980, and we are now serving the children of our

A Big Decision: Creating Your Own Sensational Cake

A lot of thought and many skilled hands are involved in the creation of a big occasion cake. Here are a few things to think about when you start planning:

1. Use this book and the cakes and recipes in it as inspiration. But also try out the recipe you want to use, from baking to decorating, at least once before the big day. Believe me, it's worth the time, energy, and money to do a test that will save you all that and more when creating the real thing.

2. If your event involves more than 50 guests,

a professional baker is essential. The baking facility should be Board of Health inspected and approved, and it must be reliable.

3. Ask for references or ask around. Nowadays, you can get feedback on message boards on the Internet about caterers and bakers.

4. Samples of cakes and fillings should be available for tasting and selection.

5. Diagrams should be made of the proposed cake design and décor and presented to you so that

but they're actually traditional; those who look traditional may want to go wild. It's up to me to find out what customers want by talking and observing to get a feeling about what might appeal to them. For example, I might ask a bride if there is a detail she loves on her dress—a swatch of lace or embroidery that might translate well on a cake. Think about where you want the sugar flowers placed. Should they be on one of the tiers or just on the top? Do you want the

> The ceremony of cutting the cake should be done early in the evening. Cake should be served as dessert after the main course with coffee or champagne. Not all guests want to party for hours on end.

you can make an informed decision.

6. Before signing a contract, make a decision about the colors and the variety of sugar floral decorations to be used on the cake. Do not use real flowers on or in the cake because they often have been sprayed with insecticides.

When it comes to the design, you should have some idea of what you want. Bring photos of what appeals to you when you meet with your cake maker. Some people want to be offbeat

flowers to trail around the cake or do you prefer clusters or a wreath effect on the tiers?

I also ask, "What flowers do you like?" For brides, it is helpful to know what flowers are in her bouquet, and I ask if her florist can email a photo or drawing of what it will look like.

My advice to brides is: Don't overspend. Money can buy a beautiful wedding, but it can't buy a good marriage, which is a journey— hopefully a long and enjoyable one.

Cake Rituals

The big day arrives, the cake is delivered, and now other decisions arise, such as where to place it and when to cut and serve it. At most functions, there is a cocktail party where guests mix and mingle and enjoy refreshments before entering the main ballroom. This is a good moment to give the cake top billing and place it in a prominent spot so guests can view it. Sometimes it is placed near the dance floor or close to the dais where the guest of honor or wedding party sits. No matter where the cake is displayed, the ceremony of cutting the cake should be done early in the evening. The perfect time is while everyone is waiting for their main course. The cake can be wheeled onto the dance floor, a little welcome speech can be made, and the guest of honor takes the first cut or the wedding couple cuts it together; the cake is then wheeled into the back and portioned and plated while the main course is served. Cake should be served as dessert after the main course with coffee or champagne. I caution couples not to wait until the end of the party to serve the cake, which might be too late. I personally rarely last to the late-night cake cutting. Not all guests want to party for hours on end.

One small aside: it's my feeling that we serve too much food. Nobody eats that much anymore. I think it's our insecurity; we feel we have to show off to impress our guests. If there's a tradition of ostentation, there's usually no turning back. Ideally, a tradition should have emotional meaning for those involved with it.

One tradition I absolutely love is saving the top tier of the wedding cake for the couple's first anniversary. In order to do this, the top tier should be removed and placed in a freezer for an hour. When the icing has hardened, the cake should be wrapped in plastic wrap and placed in an airtight plastic bag and returned to the freezer for storage until the day before the first anniversary. On that day, it should be unwrapped and allowed to defrost so it's ready for the celebration.

Brides preserve the sugar flowers from the top of their cakes by placing them under a glass dome (this one is from Tribbles in New York City). Years later, they often return to ask us to duplicate the flowers on another milestone cake.

Purity & Perfection

A Tower of Roses

YOU MIGHT ASK WHERE THE REAL ROSES STOP AND THE SUGAR ONES BEGIN. EVEN UP CLOSE, GUESTS COULDN'T TELL THE DIFFERENCE UNTIL THEY STOPPED TO SMELL THE ROSES AND ENJOY THE GUESSING GAME.

Left: Scenes from a wedding setup. I get a rush from getting the details just so. Opposite: I challenge you to tell the difference between the fresh roses and our sugar ones, each painstakingly constructed by hand with a great deal of skill and patience.

IMPROVISE: IT'S A LESSON I LIKE TO TEACH BRIDES. IT TAKES A LITTLE—SOMETIMES A LOT—OF INGENUITY TO CREATE SOMETHING SPECIAL. SO ALWAYS USE YOUR BRAINS TO GET IT JUST THE WAY YOU WANT IT.

Ingenuity and talent go into every flower we make, and for this wedding we made thousands of sugar roses of different shapes and sizes by hand. Every flower has a look—what we call a face—and if you stamp them out by machine, they'll all have the same look. We make them appear true to life, and each one is unique, whether it's the turn of the petal or the way the blossoms are put together.

The day we delivered this enormous confection, we discovered it didn't fit under the crystal chandelier where the bride wanted it placed—it was too tall for the space. All our creativity was put to the test. We realized if we removed the center of the chandelier, the cake could sit just below it and would look ethereal—as if it were soaring into the crystals above. What a great solution! Certainly, we could have panicked. But I tell brides to remember there's always a way to get through what may seem like a disaster. The trick is to not lose your composure, use a little ingenuity, and try to surround yourself with wonderful people to help you through the angst of the day.

Petal Perfect

HOW DELICIOUS! IMAGINE A LUSH
GARDEN OF HUNDREDS OF WHITE
ROSES ALL IN SUGAR, BLOSSOMING
FOR A SPRING WEDDING.

THIS IS THE SWEETEST ASSEMBLY LINE YOU'LL EVER SEE: FOR A WEDDING IN IRELAND, WE MADE AND TRANSPORTED 450 MINI-CAKES OVERSEAS.

Tradition suggests giving a small gift commemorating the day to guests attending a wedding, and through the years, these wedding favors have taken many forms. One of the sweetest tokens of affection is a mini-cake. I love the challenge of creating these cakes that must fit into a small box, yet still have a wow factor. Believe me, even though these pretty treats are tiny compared to a full-size cake, the same kind of creativity, effort, and love we put into a big cake goes into them as well.

These white rose confections were delicious, inside and out. The cake itself was a fruitcake with figs, prunes, raisins, apricots, and dates soaked in French brandy, a wise choice because fruitcakes have more longevity than the normal yellow or

white cake. As the bakers in my studio were carefully pouring the batter into miniature molds and heating the ovens, the flower makers were assembling the blossoms. Vilna Peters, who oversees the custom-flower team, has a great eye and ensures that each rose is botanically correct; she also knows how to rally the forces so everything is petal perfect right on time.

Timing really is everything in my studio, but we never take shortcuts. Each cake was iced, adorned with a sugar rose, slipped into a box, and tied with a white satin bow. When we have a massive order like this one, we all pitch in: I found myself at 8 A.M. one morning packing mini-cakes in order to make the flight departure time!

Teamwork is the real secret behind creating sensational cakes, big or small. Through planning and smart packing, each of these confections arrived in beautiful condition on the big day. Because the ceremony was in Ireland, the bride chose fruitcake for the wedding favors, so the inside was as scrumptious as the outside.

It's Spring!

I'M A FOOD PERSON. I WANT YOU TO EAT
AND ENJOY A CAKE, BUT FIRST I WANT
YOU TO FEAST YOUR EYES. THIS CALLA
LILY CAKE IS THE ESSENCE OF SPRING.
DOES IT SING TO YOU? IT SINGS TO ME.

Clockwise from top left: When we do a sketch, we scribble notes like "moth orchids, vine-y" as reminders of what the bride liked. The cake is boxed up in our workroom for its final destination. Each handmade blossom is carefully placed on the cake. Opposite: One of my talented artists, Emily Roediger-Philpot, puts a touch of red on a sugar cymbidium orchid.

A calla lily always signals springtime, and this white cake features calla lilies, tulips, hydrangeas, and berries with a wonderful peony on top. The flowers trail down and around on the cake—it's a style we've done for years. But you know something? People never tire of it. A classic is always going to be there, because it's absolutely beautiful. After all, it's not just a cake; it's a whole experience. I want you to have all the sensations when you look at one of my cakes. I want your palate to enjoy it, your heart to sing, and your memory of it to last. Sometimes memory is better than the real thing!

Of course, everything on this cake is sugar, even the cymbidium orchid that my artist is painting. The orchid has a throat, so we put some exciting color on it as a surprise, just like in nature. When you look at that cake and all of its perfect little details, you want to say, "I love it! This says 'spring!'"

Cake decorators often use pastry tubes and tips to make icing flowers, but we use sugar dough so ours will be beautifully realistic down to the veins on the fragile petals. A sugar phalaenopsis moth orchid is indistinguishable from its real counterpart up close, or from a distance (opposite), sitting in its all-sugar cake terra-cotta planter.

Center of Attention

A LOT HAPPENS AROUND THE CAKE. WEDDINGS ARE
FILLED WITH RITUALS THAT CELEBRATE THE
JOY OF THE BIG DAY, AND IT'S NOT SURPRISING
THAT THESE MOMENTS—FROM WELCOMING GUESTS
TO TAKING PHOTOS—TAKE PLACE
NEARBY THIS TOWER OF SUGAR FLOWERS.

RITUALS ARE IMPORTANT AT A WEDDING. BRIDES OFTEN ASK ME HOW THEY SHOULD HANDLE THE MOMENT WHEN THEY PRESENT AND CUT THE CAKE.

Too often, the tradition of the bride and groom cutting the cake is delayed until after dinner. That is a mistake. The cake should be part of the dinner and should follow the main course. I frequently suggest that the couple toast their guests and welcome them to the ceremonial event, cut the cake, and then have their first wedded dance while the cake is removed to be cut for dessert. This gives everyone the opportunity to join in on the dance floor and then take their seats for dinner. That way, there is plenty of time for the cake to be sliced, portioned on plates, and served properly as dessert.

The cake ritual is a lot of fun and can be wonderful, as long as the

couple doesn't decide to get a little wicked when they're feeding each other a slice. After all, it's a ritual that signals the beginning of sharing a life together. The couple shares a piece of cake—food, which is the essence of life. As for logistics, I think slicing it together with two hands on the knife does the job beautifully. Some brides choose a special cake knife to commemorate the moment, but I'd be careful about using an heirloom. In the excitement of the evening, it might get lost unless there's someone in the wedding party who is responsible for it. A wedding should be the beginning—not the end—of family traditions.

Left to right: This stunning flower-covered cake was placed at the front of the room near the stage for all to admire. The young couple enjoyed the ritual of cutting the cake and sharing a slice. Many of the details, including the ring pillow, picked up the lush flowers in the centerpieces that are also echoed on the cake. Harriet Rose Katz, a wonderful event planner, orchestrated this wedding fantasy.

The Happy
Bride's Bouquet

OH, IT'S BEAUTIFUL! THIS HAPPY BRIDE WANTED
HER CAKE TO REFLECT THE GORGEOUS FLOWERS
AND DELICATE FERNS IN HER WONDERFUL BOUQUET.

LET ME TELL YOU ABOUT THIS ONE. WE MADE THE CAKE SQUARE—AND SQUARE BECAUSE IT'S DIFFERENT, BUT STILL CONVENTIONAL, WHICH IS WHAT MOST BRIDES WANT.

Every bride is different, and finding the perfect cake for each one is like figuring out which hairdo will complement her features best. The bride who ordered this scrumptious cake was such a happy bride—she was not what we call a difficult lady (and you do get difficult ladies). She was just divine. The bouquets were very clean and very beautiful in shades of soft pink, but when we talked, she told me she wanted something that was like a garden and a bit earthy to pick up the feeling of the maidenhair fern in her bouquet. It's delicate and fragile, just like the bride, who was very young, very beautiful, and very delicate.

So we filled her cake bouquet with all the prettiest sugar flowers—roses, orchids, peonies, and hydrangeas, with purple sugar irises here and there. It turned out as gorgeous and approachable as the girl herself and worked well in the party room with its long, long table.

If you look closely at the photos, you can see people staring at the cake. Guests photographed themselves next to it, and you can see a woman in blue with a look on her face that says, "I wish it were mine!" I try to make every cake so personalized that a bride will look at it and say, "This isn't A, B, or C—this is mine."

Left to right: The square cake with its tempting sugar flowers and lace cutouts copies the look of the embroidery on the bride's wedding gown. Fresh pink flowers were used in the place settings. A bridesmaid's bouquet holds roses, maidenhair ferns, and hydrangea. I like long tables; if you dine at a table like this, you have six people you can talk to very easily—one on either side of you and four across. With a big round table, you have to shout, but with this kind of setup, you can speak to almost everyone.

Bower of Flowers

"GOING GREEN" HAS BECOME A FASHIONABLE CATCHPHRASE, BUT THIS WEDDING COUPLE TOOK THE SENTIMENT TO HEART WITH A SIMPLE WHITE CAKE WITH SUGAR FERNS AND DOGWOOD.

Not every bride wants an extravagant wedding reception in a big ballroom. I applaud those who are happy with a low-key affair, and I make every effort to come up with a wedding cake that beautifully reflects the bride's interests and desires. We occasionally get a request for a cake with organic ingredients, and my studio is as eco-friendly as I am. My brides always get a fresh, delicious cake because we start with the best materials available. I've always been opposed to putting real flowers on a cake, because most of the time these flowers have been sprayed with insecticide—or they may hide a bug under a leaf or petal. A bug is just the kind of guest you don't want at your wedding, indoors or out.

The young couple planned an outdoor wedding with close friends and family, and hoped for beautiful weather so that everyone could enjoy a slice of cake and a glass of champagne in the spring air. Their Garden of Eden was a dark wood gazebo surrounded with ivy and lush ferns; a striped green-and-white tablecloth and fern-filled bouquet of peonies and miniature roses set the stage for the refreshments. The simple white cake we created mirrored the unpretentious spirit of the day with sugar dogwood blossoms and sugar fern fronds that look just the way Mother Nature intended.

Pick a color theme that complements the natural surroundings. That's what my friend Carolyne Roehm did for this simple affair, and you can see how effectively the idea works. The striped tablecloth plays off the profusion of greenery and works with the cake topped with white sugar dogwood and pale green sugar ferns.

Poetry in Motion

EXQUISITE SUGAR FLOWERS ON
AN ELEGANT WEDDING CAKE
TRAVEL WELL WHEN TREATED
WITH TENDER LOVING CARE.

WEDDING CAKES ARE LIKE MAGICAL CREATURES: THEY APPEAR OUT OF NOWHERE IN A TOWER OF PERFECTION TO SURPRISE EVERYONE WITH THEIR BEAUTY. SO WHETHER WE TRAVEL TWO BLOCKS OR TWO CONTINENTS AWAY WHEN DELIVERING OUR CAKES, WE MAKE SURE EACH BLOSSOM ARRIVES IN THE MOST BEAUTIFUL CONDITION.

The all-white wedding cake is considered by some the traditional route to go for a formal wedding. Some may even consider an all-white cake the safest, most boring choice to make—but I'd hardly call this amazing Eiffel Tower of a wedding cake ho-hum. For one thing, the sugar flowers are breathtaking! The sheer height of it fit the surroundings and complemented the ornate décor.

Diary of a wedding cake: The sketch looks a little abstract, but the annotations fill in all the details. Tiers are packed in separate boxes to be decorated upon arrival. Handle with care? We cross our fingers, hoping cargo handlers at Continental, our carrier of choice, will heed our "this way up" arrows. Opposite: Michele Gemin, one of my beloved staffers, readies the cake. I always pack my "doctor's bag" with extra flowers, buttercream, and utensils, to repair anything damaged in transit.

My cakes have traveled farther than I have in the world. Sometimes I go with them, when my schedule allows, and in this instance I boarded an international flight to shepherd the twenty boxes needed to ship this skyscraper of a cake (plus 450 wedding favor cakes) for a spectacular wedding in Ireland. Sometimes, when I board a plane, I say to the pilot, "You have a wedding cake on board! Don't brake hard. Avoid turbulence. And please glide when you land." We always put arrows on the boxes so cargo handlers know which way is up, and sometimes the crew will meet us in the baggage claim to ask, "How did it land?" That's when I realize the importance of a wedding cake—like a celebrity or the queen, it's always given the V.I.P. treatment no matter where it goes.

GUESTS LOOK FORWARD TO THE SWEET MOMENT WHEN A WEDDING CAKE IS SERVED. WITH THE RIGHT CHOICE, YOU'LL HAVE THE CAKE OF YOUR DREAMS.

I always ask couples to come to my studio for a tasting, so I can explain what choices they have for a cake. I present our thirteen flavors of fillings on a smooth white painter's palette first: There's vanilla, key lime, lemon, blood orange, chocolate mousse, apricot, hazelnut, strawberry, pistachio, raspberry, coconut, caramel, and mocha espresso. I tell the couple to take a fork, have a little taste, and see what intrigues them. I encourage them to experiment and mix flavors. They might try chocolate, vanilla, and caramel together—or blood orange, lemon, or strawberry with chocolate and vanilla.

What most people don't realize is that each tier has four

layers, so each slice of cake has three fillings. The fillings can be the same or combinations that work, like vanilla, chocolate, and lemon—or two raspberries and one lemon. With the berry fillings, you get fresh sliced fruit, too. After tasting the fillings, the couple samples the cake and chooses between vanilla, yellow buttercake, or two kinds of chocolate cake. My advice is to put fruity fillings with yellow buttercake; chocolate, vanilla, and raspberry with chocolate cake; and have two variations, so every guest has a choice. Surprisingly, no one feels overwhelmed because I make it fun— serious fun, yes, but isn't that the best kind there is?

Dreams come true, left to right: Monograms are a way to make a wedding cake unique. This five-tier cake has a cascade of sugar flowers, including roses and cherry blossoms, and a monogram with the couple's initials. A traditional all-white cake has gorgeous wreaths of flowers and piping to set it apart from more conventional treatments.

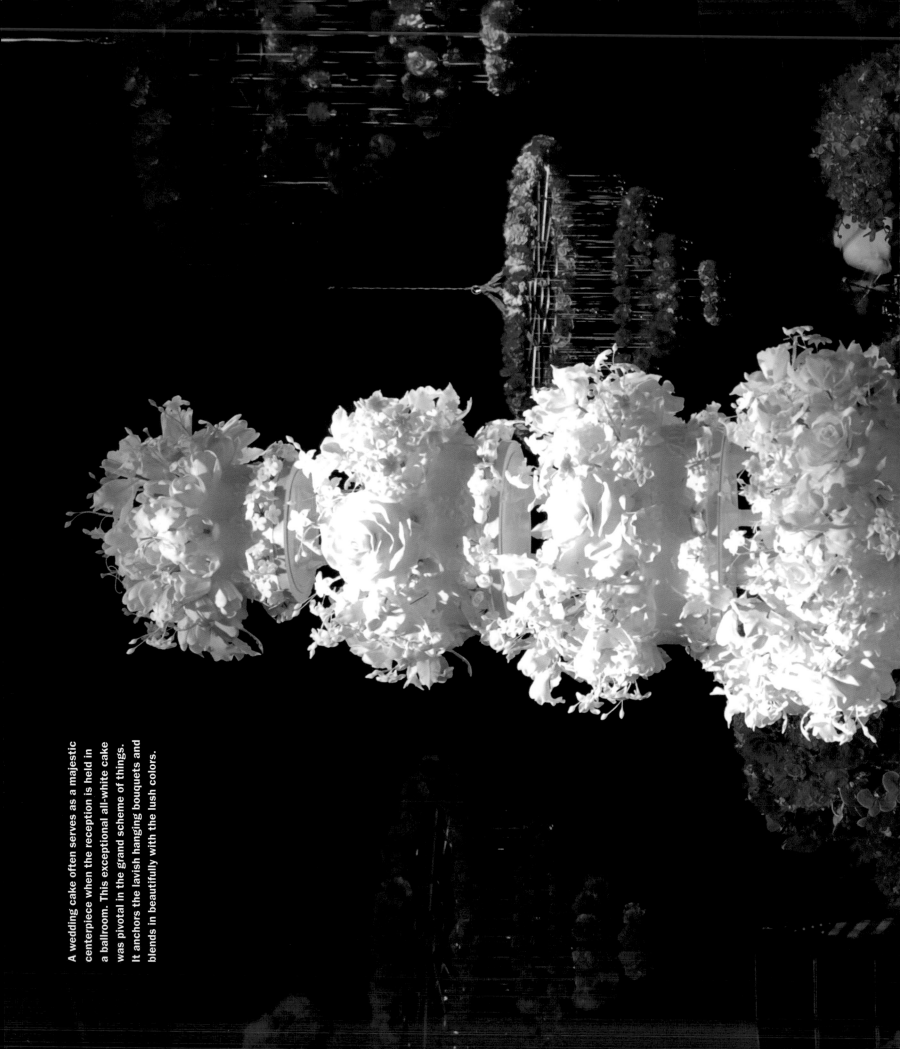

A wedding cake often serves as a majestic centerpiece when the reception is held in a ballroom. This exceptional all-white cake was pivotal in the grand scheme of things. It anchors the lavish hanging bouquets and blends in beautifully with the lush colors.

A Touch
of Blue

*A Kiss
from a Rose*

AT AN ELEGANT WEDDING IN NEWPORT,
EVERYONE HAD A WONDERFUL TIME,
ESPECIALLY THE YOUNG COUPLE,
WHO REQUESTED LOTS OF ROMANTIC
FLOWERS ON THEIR SCRUMPTIOUS CAKE.

ROSES, ROSEBUDS, HYDRANGEAS,
AND SWEETPEAS—WHAT A
GORGEOUS COMBINATION OF
FLOWERS FOR THE SUGAR BOUQUET
ON TOP OF A WEDDING CAKE!

People always ask me: Where do you get your inspiration for a cake? For this wedding it was easy: The bride loved the pearl embroidery on the waistband of her gown, which also had ruches in the back that looked amazing when she danced. We re-created the embroidery on alternating tiers of the cake.

The colors used were equally remarkable. The buttercream icing was tinted a soft blue to match the colors in the room—a most unusual look! The hydrangeas and sweet peas were steel blue, the roses a pale peach, and the combination created a very sophisticated palette that worked well with the décor. The gold chairs were unadorned, and the centerpieces on the round tables were topiary-style clusters of white blossoms. It was a great example of what I call "affordable luxury." There was nothing ostentatious about it at all.

Take a lesson from this lovely bride and splurge on a few things. Not everything needs to be over the top! Her gown had exquisite embroidery (above), which was then reflected in the five-tier wedding cake (above center). The unusual colors made the cake a focal point at the reception, which was decorated in a spare, elegant way. As you can see, the couple enjoyed several delicious moments at their party!

Pretty embroidery, like this beautiful handwork on an Anne Barge gown, can serve as inspiration for a detail on a cake. Opposite: The ornate beading on this Reem Acra gown was replicated on the cake. The source of the embellishment was revealed when the bride in her lovely gown stood next to her wedding cake.

In Love with Lace

ANYTHING CAN BE INSPIRING!
I OFTEN ASK A BRIDE TO SEND
ME A SWATCH OF FABRIC OR LACE
FROM HER GOWN TO HELP ME
DESIGN THE TEXTURE OF THE
ICING WHEN I PREPARE A
SKETCH FOR HER CAKE.

AT A SIMPLE OUTDOOR
WEDDING, THE SUN
WAS SHINING, THE BRIDE
WAS BEAUTIFUL, AND
PALE BLUE WAS THE
ORDER OF THE DAY.

The young bride, who had exquisite taste, adored the lace on her strapless gown and liked the idea of having it as the detail on the wedding cake. Lace is beautiful, and when it's done in buttercream, it translates into a beautiful finish on the cake. (Yes, these details are buttercream on buttercream, so people can actually eat it.) And since pale blue was one of the themes of the party—the bridesmaids all wore that shade—we chose it as the border on the cake. Blue and white has a lovely feeling to it, doesn't it? It's a very simple but very elegant look. It's not overdone.

As you can see, the little take-home gifts were also deliciously unpretentious. Everything came together in this wedding, from gown to cake to giveaways—and how nice that Mother Nature provided the matching blue sky.

Left to right: After the ceremony, guests took their places at tables set up outside. Lacy vines and flowers decorate the four-tiered cake with small bouquets of white sugar roses and rosebuds. A bouquet of deep pink roses looks fresh and appealing. Iced cookies wrapped in cellophane and tied with a blue ribbon carried out the color scheme.

Tied with a Bow

AT A BRIDAL SHOWER BRUNCH, MINIATURE CAKES END THE PARTY ON A SWEET, CHIC NOTE.

Lily of the valley is a favorite flower of brides, and we often get requests to include these bell-shaped blossoms on wedding cakes. The delicate white blooms were just the right touch on the mini dessert cakes we made for a bridal shower designed by Carolyne Roehm that had a blue-and-white theme.

Created to look like two-tiered wedding cakes, each polka-dot layer was tied with a navy and white saddle-stitched bow—all in sugar, of course. Atop this scrumptious little confection was a sugary sprig of lily of the valley. What made these affordable luxuries even more wonderful in my eyes was that they were made of lemon cake and fresh raspberries—my favorite combination!

The inspiration behind this sophisticated color scheme was Coco Chanel, who used navy and white in her legendary designs. Every detail was thought out in advance, from the quilted paper and saddle-stitch bows that echo the legendary quilted Chanel bags, to the singular miniature cakes that we created for dessert.

Forget Me Not

I THINK IT'S IMPORTANT TO ENJOY YOURSELF
IN LIFE. PARTIES BRING PEOPLE TOGETHER AND
HOPEFULLY THEY HAVE A MEMORABLE TIME—LIKE THE
GUESTS DID AT THIS WONDERFUL SPRING WEDDING.

THIS WAS THE
WEDDING OF A
SOPHISTICATED
COUPLE WHO
WANTED TO KEEP
THINGS SIMPLE—
ALL IN A PALETTE
OF BLUE AND WHITE.
THEY HAD BEEN
TO MANY WEDDINGS
AND SEEN LOTS OF
FROUFROU, BUT
DECIDED THAT THE
LOOK OF THEIRS
WOULD BE CLEAN
AND MODERN, BUT
ROMANTIC AT
THE SAME TIME.

The wedding reception was a
luncheon at a beautiful place on Park
Avenue that used to be a church.
The site often dictates the décor,
and originally, the florist wanted
to use shades of blue into lavender
for the arrangements. But the bride
and her mother were adamant about
using white and just one shade of
blue on everything—they didn't want
variations—as you can see.

Far left: There I am, adding the finishing touches. There are hundreds of people orchestrating a major event—it's a scene behind a scene. Some do the flowers, and others provide the food, the valet service, and all the nitty-gritty stuff (like these gift boxes, left). I don't know if people know what goes into this theater of life or if brides realize that so many people who are a part of their event share the joy. Opposite: Even the domed ceiling picked up on the blue and white theme.

CAKES REPRESENT MANY THINGS. CAKES ARE FOOD, AND FOOD IS SEX AND LOVE, TOO. WHAT I WANT TO DO IS CREATE ARTISTIC FOOD TO EXCITE YOUR PALATE, BUT ALSO APPEAL TO YOUR EYES AND YOUR SOUL. I WANT YOU TO BE ECSTATIC WHEN YOU SEE OUR CAKES.

Forget-me-nots, hydrangea, lilies of the valley, and spirea were the sugar flowers chosen for the cake at this elegant wedding. The couple felt no need for things to be grand. There are people who love extravagant events, but others prefer something more intimate so that they can get to know people. At a grand event, you just move through a wonderful party filled with women in beautiful gowns and men in tuxes—that's what big weddings are about. You don't know all the guests—it's like the beginning of the telephone book—and that's okay. But for our birthdays and major anniversaries, my husband and I don't even celebrate—we disappear, just the two of us, with a set of pajamas, a good bottle of champagne, and some caviar. That's what we did for our fiftieth anniversary, and we'll continue to do that.

A wow of a wedding: This spectacular cake had many tiers and thousands of sugar roses on it. It sat in a tall atrium on a pool of water with a row of candles and a waterfall behind it and a row of smaller white cakes in front.

Go with the Flow

A BIAS CUT ON A WEDDING GOWN IS
A FLATTERING DETAIL, AND WHEN DONE
IN SUGAR, IT'S JUST AS DELICIOUS—
AS YOU CAN SEE ON THIS GORGEOUS CAKE.

VERY FEW PEOPLE HAVE A PERFECT BODY, AND IN A BEAUTIFUL SILK SATIN WEDDING GOWN, A BIAS CUT FLOWS OVER THE BODY'S CURVES. ON A CAKE, A SILKY DRAPE DONE IN SUGAR ADDS A PERSONAL, ALLURING TOUCH.

For this wedding cake, I copied the drape of the bride's satin gown in sugar, so it looks as delectable as the silky detail of the dress. When the bride stands next to her cake, you know right away she's the inspiration. This was a spring cake, and the bride loved shades of lavender. On her dress, the satin was caught at her shoulder with a cluster of silk hydrangeas, and then draped over the bosom, with a bouquet of blossoms at her waist. Isn't it amazing! The blossoms on this cake are like Lesage embroidery on a Chanel couture gown. I have been called the Lesage of cakes, because the artists in my studio are as talented as the embroiderers in that Parisian atelier. What we do when we create a beautiful cake is labor intensive—just like the legendary artisans who work with silk thread to make an embroidered flower on an evening coat or a row of sequins on a dress to be worn on the red carpet. We are after the same thing in our work—perfection.

Left: I always sketch out what the cake will look like so brides aren't surprised by the end result. Opposite: Our cakes are not mass-produced. What we do is not done by amateurs, whether it's icing piped onto the cake, or leaves, shells, or blossoms, all created by hand in sugar. If you want quality, you go for the real thing.

Let's Talk Lavender

I ALWAYS TELL BRIDES, THERE IS NO SUCH
THING AS TRADITIONAL—IT'S SIMPLY
ABOUT WHAT YOU LIKE. IT'S EASY TO
SEE WHAT COLOR THIS BRIDE PREFERRED!

A BRIDAL BOUQUET IS OFTEN A SOURCE OF INSPIRATION WHEN IT COMES TO CREATING THE LOOK OF A WEDDING CAKE. THE FIRST QUESTION I ASK THE BRIDE IS, "ARE THERE FLOWERS YOU PARTICULARLY LIKE?"

Sometimes a couple will come to me and say they want a traditional-looking cake. Traditional? I ask. I remind them that there are many traditions in the world and beautiful ones at that, but this is their wedding. It's what they like that's important, and in my first meeting with them, I always ask lots of questions and try to find out their preferences—what they think is perfect or just so-so.

This bride loved lavender and was planning to use the color in a big way—for her bridesmaids' dresses, in her bouquet, for the centerpieces, and, of course, on the wedding cake. I explained how important it is to balance out the colors because a strong shade on a white cake can photograph spotty, which won't look pretty in a picture. My suggestion was to lighten it up with white and light green. Peach tulips, creamy roses with a hint of pink, and leaves were set next to sprigs of violet and purple hydrangea. When designing a color scheme for a cake, I also consider the time of year, the season, and the décor of the space where the event is being held. For example, if a reception is at a country club with wood paneling and heavy curtains, you lighten it up with whites, creams, yellows, or light blues. I think it worked for this wedding—and the photos prove it!

A Daisy of a Cake

YOU KNOW IT'S SUMMER WHEN YOU SEE DAISIES. FOR AN AUGUST BIRTHDAY, I DECORATED A WHITE CAKE WITH THESE HAPPY FLOWERS, GORGEOUS BLUE HYDRANGEAS, AND A SUGAR BUTTERFLY.

Blue and white with daisies—I can't think of a more appealing combination, especially in the summertime. My friend Carolyne Roehm called and said, "I need a cake for a party for two birthdays—my mom's seventy-fifth and my aunt June's eightieth." I always have a lot of freedom doing cakes for Carolyne, who trusts me to come up with something special that works with her color theme. Daisies are an open-face flower with a bright button center, and the scattering of sugar daisies on the cake blend with the daisy bouquets on the tables. But what made this cake memorable was the edible monarch butterfly taking flight on top—it's always the unexpected touch that makes a lasting impression on guests.

Utterly
Feminine

Standing Ovation

I LOVE WHEN A BRIDE WANTS A CAKE THAT'S
TALLER THAN SHE IS! WHILE A WEDDING
CAKE SHOULD NEVER UPSTAGE THE WEDDING
COUPLE, A FLOWERY BEAUTY LIKE THIS
ONE DESERVES A ROUND OF APPLAUSE.

PINK IS ONE OF THOSE OOH–LA–LA COLORS, BUT THIS EIGHT-TIERED CAKE WENT WELL BEYOND THAT ADJECTIVE. ON A GRAND SCALE, THE COLOR PINK HAS A REAL PRESENCE, SIGNALING LOVE, TENDERNESS, AND AFFECTION TO ALL.

Smart brides know you can have too much of a good thing. For example, at a big wedding brides sometimes make the mistake of having everything match, from the flowers to the bridesmaids' dresses to the tabletop linens. The result is boring! While the scale of elements in a room needs to be in proportion—like the way the wedding cake worked in tandem with the cascading centerpieces on each table at this event—there should be a lush mix of details that complement each other. That's what we tried to achieve in the flowers on this cake: Each tier was different, as was each unique blossom on it. I like to think people recognize the effort we put into each flower and in turn feel a certain joy. An occasion such as this should be filled with joy down to the smallest detail, because it celebrates the beginning of something beautiful—a life together.

Making a sweetpea: There are four stages for each blossom. First, a petal of sugar dough is cut out using a teardrop template, then smoothed with a balling tool (designed by my husband, Ben) to a paper-thin consistency. The "teardrop" is wrapped around flower wire, and gently shaped by hand into a petal shape. Rows of sweetpeas dry, then are stored in boxes, until we're ready to use them on a cake.

Grand Gets Grander

PINK REIGNED AT THIS EXTRAVAGANT AND
ELEGANT WEDDING AT THE WALDORF–ASTORIA
HOTEL. EVEN THE FOUNTAINS
COORDINATED WITH THE COLOR SCHEME.

GRAND—JUST THE WORD TELLS YOU THE
WEDDING IS GOING TO BE EXCEPTIONAL.
COUPLES OFTEN TELL ME, "MAKE IT
AS TALL AND AS SPECTACULAR AS YOU CAN.
THIS IS OUR DREAM CAKE."

Tulips, roses, sweet peas—all the romantic flowers you can think of were
used on this special wedding cake—not a dandelion in sight! The
wedding, which was for a first daughter, was held in the evening at the
Waldorf-Astoria Hotel in New York City, and it was the epitome of
formal. This event was designed by my good friend Preston Bailey.
Still, grand is in the eye of the beholder. People will say to me,
"Money is no object." My answer is, "There's always a budget." I
remember a couple who were inviting only 35 guests and wanted
the wedding to be spectacular. Everything that went into this
wedding was unusual. When you serve rare vintages and hire an
executive chef to make food that's extraordinary, and you bring in
your own furniture, china, silver, and crystal, yes, you'll spend
quite a lot. But I like the idea of affordable luxury. You can have
an intimate luncheon with your family and closest friends and
make it beautiful. Do you go into the wedding with the same
heart and love? I would rather hope so. You do the best you
can with what you have. If you have the million, spend it.
And if you have less, spend that. It can be just as wonderful.
Weddings are not always about exceptional food and
wine. They are about the celebration and how we all
get together to send off this lovely new couple
to a new life. Don't you agree?

Left: The sketch of the cake hints at its
opulence. Opposite: You don't often get to
do a wedding for an international crowd and
have the privilege of using a premier hotel
with an enormous space. For a ballroom, you
want something that makes a statement,
or else it won't be seen. If you're going to
have 500 people, you need a cake that's
appropriate for the space.

The artists in my studio use their creativity—and simple tools—to get the realistic look of the sugar flowers we put on our cakes. Notice the veins on this brilliant parrot tulip. Opposite: Brushes and dusting powders are used to enhance colors on sugar dough.

Fun at All Angles

HOW CAN A CAKE LOOK TOPSY-TURVY, YET STILL BE GLAMOROUS? IT'S ALL A MATTER OF BALANCING THE FRIVOLITY WITH THE FINER THINGS IN LIFE.

You have to have a sense of fun when you're planning a party, and a whimsical cake helps set the mood. Guests always get a kick out of a "crooked" cake. You know, this cake isn't *really* crooked—it's made to look that way. Many years ago, when I was a schoolteacher, I liked Dr. Seuss books: The illustrations were clever and charming, and if you looked at those pictures, everything was slightly askew and so whimsical. So when I got into the cake business, I wanted to do a cake inspired by the drawings in *Cat in the Hat*. I rigged up an infrastructure so the cake would sit at silly angles. In truth, the biggest problem was teaching the public to understand that it was done on purpose! Adventurous brides adore these eccentric cakes, and nowadays, the gorgeous sugar flowers on the angled tiers signal that this is a confection to be taken seriously.

This scrumptious pink cake is not for a staid or elegant party, but it injects a note of frivolity at a sophisticated, formal affair. Preston Bailey, who is an extraordinary party planner, always does things with incredible flair, and this particular cake matched the individuality of the setting and décor.

Something Old, Something New

I'M A VERY SIMPLE PERSON, NOT EASILY
IMPRESSED. BUT WHEN I SEE SOMETHING
BEAUTIFUL, I'M INSPIRED BY IT. WE FOUND
OUT THE BRIDE COLLECTED ANTIQUE PEWTER,
AND THAT'S HOW THIS CAKE WAS BORN.

ALMOST ANYTHING CAN SERVE AS AN INSPIRATION FOR A DESIGN. OFTEN THE BEST IDEAS COME STRAIGHT FROM A PERSON'S LIFE—WHAT THEY COLLECT, WHERE THEY'VE TRAVELED, OR WHEN THEY FIRST FELL IN LOVE.

What's great about making cakes is learning about people and their lives. For this cake, we got to know the bride and what she liked to collect—old pewter. I always like to incorporate something personal in the design to make it unique and memorable for the family. An artist in my shop created a pewter teapot out of Styrofoam to sit on top of the cake so the whole thing could be removed—sugar flowers and all. These flowers are as beautiful as real ones, but they last. I'm against using real flowers on a cake because as they grow they're sprayed with insecticide. Plus, they can bring in ants—not what you want at a wedding! I've found that some brides keep our flowers forever. Women who were married 25 years ago return with the flowers from their wedding cakes to use as inspiration for their child's sixteenth birthday cake or a son's engagement party. That's what's great about being in business for almost 30 years—I see people again and again, at different stages of their lives and during their happiest occasions.

Opposite, clockwise from top left: The lattice effect on the cake worked well in the informal setting. (I would never advise this for a formal ballroom!) However, I am here to please the bride. If she truly wants basketweave or lattice, so be it. The handmade butterfly, a symbol of luck and love, and the tiny caterpillar represented two beloved guests who were unable to attend. Close-ups of the leaves, roses, peonies, and tendrils display the artistry of the handwork done by my talented flower makers.

Each sugar flower we create takes several steps: This pale pink peony is in the early stage of being "built" from the center stamens out to the delicate, ruffled petals. Opposite: You can see the imprint of our work in the natural look of the frilly petals of this peony.

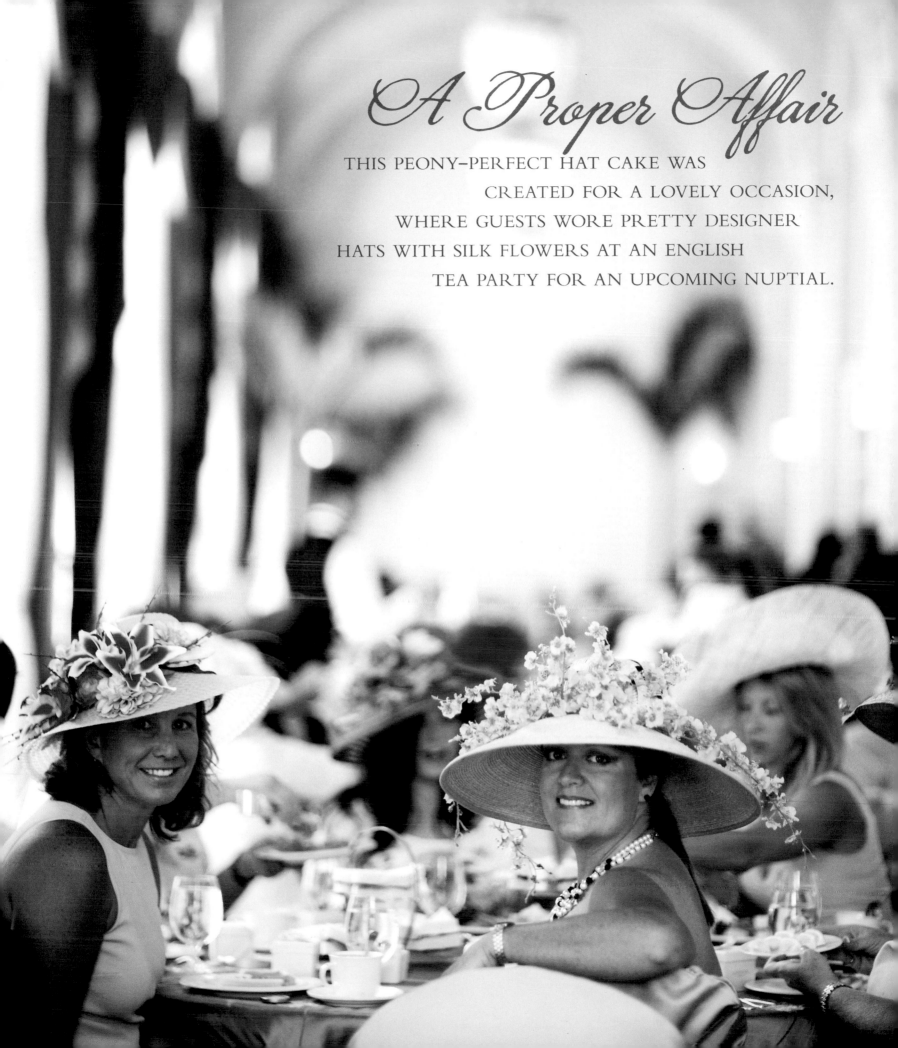

A Proper Affair

THIS PEONY-PERFECT HAT CAKE WAS
CREATED FOR A LOVELY OCCASION,
WHERE GUESTS WORE PRETTY DESIGNER
HATS WITH SILK FLOWERS AT AN ENGLISH
TEA PARTY FOR AN UPCOMING NUPTIAL.

EVEN GROWNUPS LIKE TO PLAY DRESS-UP, AND PARTIES ARE A GOOD TIME TO INDULGE IN THAT FANTASY. EVERY DETAIL—FROM THE SETTING TO THE SWEETS THE GUESTS TOOK HOME—CONTRIBUTED TO THE EFFECT.

I like it when someone has a spirit of adventure. After all, the best times come out of a willingness to try something new. A luncheon for out-of-town guests was planned, and the young woman wanted to do an English tea at a hotel with a conservatory look. Hats from a local designer were commissioned, and everyone wore one. (And why not? They were irresistible!) Lunch was served, and instead of traditional scones with strawberry jam or little cakes, the hostess liked the idea of having a dessert that would suit the theme of the party. I created a cake in the shape of a hat, and the artists in my shop made the prettiest sugar flowers—peonies, lilies, sweet peas, and rosebuds—to adorn it; their artistry was matched only by the silk flowers on the big brimmed hats. When dessert was brought out, guests applauded not only the cake, but the hostess's ingenuity and effort as well.

Scenes from an English tea: This was the actual hat (above left) that inspired the scrumptious cake made for the event. When you compare the sugar hat with the real one, you see how the artistry of my staff shows up in all of the details, from the ribbons on the hat to the sugar flowers trimming it. It's clear we all had lots of fun wearing the spectacular hats and how elegant, yet comfortable, the conservatory setting looked for the afternoon luncheon.

The artists in my studio often consult photographs of flowers in order to capture the subtle gradation of color or marking on a pansy, for instance. Opposite: Note how there is an imprint on these miniature orchids, created by the fine lines on the hand of the artist who made them.

Sugar dough butterflies take flight on an individual mini cake. These little cakes look spectacular lined up for a luncheon or special afternoon tea. Opposite: A close-up shows how realistic the details are on a sugar dough butterfly.

Bright & Happy

Teacup Cake

IMAGINE THE IMPACT OF A TABLE
SET WITH A DOZEN OF THESE SWEET
SURPRISES FOR A BIRTHDAY LUNCHEON.

I often say, "Some joy is cooking when we come up with a great idea and, oh boy, isn't someone going to be happy with the outcome?" Never say never. At least that's how I feel whenever someone asks for the impossible—like making tiny teacup cakes designed from favorite pieces of china. These precious desserts emulate two different styles: One is a bright yellow cup with blue birds and gold details; the other is a majolica design from Portugal. Both are happy patterns because of the bold yellow, blue, and white palette—and the artists in my shop easily translated the artistry on each of the teacups onto the miniature desserts.

One big cake, beautifully decorated, can have a lot of impact, especially if it's placed to act as a focal point in a room. The cake should also be well lit so the colors on it stand out. But a row of little beauties will make a simple table into a fancy one—you don't even need real flowers! There's also something very special about treating guests to their own individual cakes—especially a fantasy dessert like these flower-filled ones. You'll be surprised that even the dieters in the crowd will happily indulge. Tell them to forget the calorie count, for once—and enjoy an edible work of art.

Real or sugar? You guess. These miniatures emulate the actual china teacups so closely that sometimes guests are afraid to eat them! The artists in my shop make each of the miniature hydrangea and phlox blossoms by hand, petal by petal, and paint the details with edible food coloring.

Long ago, when I first started creating sugar flowers, I'd go to the florist and buy a single bloom of whatever I wanted to make and then take it apart to figure out the precise configuration. These poppy buds reflect that lifelong desire to make sugar flowers look as realistic and beautiful as possible.

The menu card reads:

Cajun Dinner at Greendune

Napoleon of Fried Green Tomatoes

Memphis Fried Oysters

Jalapeno Cornbread

Louisiana Jambalaya

Chicory Salad with Pecan Mustard Vinaigrette

Leo Celebration Cakes

Casal Garcia Vinho Verde

Marqués de Riscal Rioja 1997

Sweet and Sunny

SUNFLOWERS WERE THE THEME OF A SUMMER SOIREE, AND EACH GUEST GOT THEIR OWN LITTLE GLORIOUS CAKE WITH THIS BRIGHT MOTIF.

Sunflowers are a happy flower, just like daisies. You feel good when you see one. At this birthday party thrown at the height of summer, there were big bunches of sunflowers everywhere: near the bar, on the black-and-white-striped lunch table, in enormous black urns by the pool, and as a single note on the menu card at each place setting. Even still, guests were pleasantly surprised when they were each presented with a sugar sunflower on a dessert cake iced in white and black frosting to match the décor. While a large cake decorated with sunflowers would also have been impressive, these scrumptious ones made guests feel special. Try this idea for a special dinner party—think of it as an affordable luxury—and treat your guests to their own brilliant blooms.

Above: Carolyne Roehm, who planned this chic party, has great taste and knows exactly how to use beautiful flowers to great effect. Right: These mini-squares were made of almond cake with basic buttercream icing. I love how open and inviting the sunflowers look—they're like faces. In the South of France, I remember passing a field of them all turned toward the sun—and then on our trip back noticing how they had turned the other way as the sun moved across the sky.

You'll need to look twice to tell the difference between the sugar and the real tulips. Opposite: Phlox, lilac, hydrangea, stephanotis, and orange blossoms are what we call "spray flowers" because we bunch sprays of them together on a stem.

A Rosy Beginning

SOME BRIDES CONSIDER A WEDDING THE
MOST IMPORTANT TIME OF THEIR LIVES, BUT
IT IS NOT. THIS JOYFUL CELEBRATION IS JUST
THE BEGINNING OF A WHOLE NEW LIFE.
I ALWAYS WANT COUPLES TO HAVE THE MOST
BEAUTIFUL CAKE FOR THIS HAPPY MOMENT.

NOT EVERY CAKE WE DO IS EXTRAVAGANT, BUT EACH IS BEAUTIFUL IN ITS OWN WAY. THIS PARTICULAR CAKE IS AN AFFORDABLE LUXURY AND WILL FEED 150 PEOPLE EASILY.

Yellow and orange are such happy, warm colors. The moment you see a cake like this, you know it's not the dead of winter. For this couple, we created the lightest, most beautiful cake. Those are real petals around the base; they coordinate with the sugar flowers on the cake and the bouquets on the table. I don't mind them at all because the colors work with the cake. I would mind them if they were the wrong colors. But we spoke to the florist and he coordinated the look with us. When you look at the room, it reads warmth. It's very happy. You see the wonderful bouquets are not tight tussy mussies; they're loose and full. They look happy, just like the cake.

You know, the cake is such an integral part of a wedding. It may very well be the highlight or focal point of it—the last word, you might say. The cake stands alone, and people pose in front of it to take photos. At certain moments, it's as important as the bride—but what about the groom? Make sure to make your groom happy and get him a slice, I tell the brides. Without him, we don't have a wedding! I always encourage couples to save the cake's top section for their first anniversary. Sharing it helps them realize the importance of being together and how that closeness can continue long after the wedding party.

Left: Can you tell the sugar flowers from the real ones? Roses, calla lilies, peonies, and orchids were all made by hand, petal by petal. **Opposite:** The flowers for this cake took around 300 hours and the talents of 20 people to create. Without the team, it doesn't happen.

A still-life with freesias, faux and real. Opposite: Our sugar bouquets can be lifted right off the cake to be displayed in a clear box or used as a centerpiece or the top of a topiary.

Sugar dough, also known as sugar paste or gum paste, is what we use in my studio to make flowers, ruffles, ribbons, and drapes. Every petal and leaf on this magnificent cake is completely edible—which is one of my rules for a cake. I never like using fresh flowers, because most are sprayed with insecticides or fumigated while they're growing. Some flowers are also poisonous—and you certainly don't want to poison your guests!

Passionate Hues

A Feast for the Senses

A CAKE SHOULD WOW YOU WITH ITS
COLOR AND AMAZING DETAILS THE MINUTE
YOU SEE IT, EVEN FROM ACROSS THE ROOM.

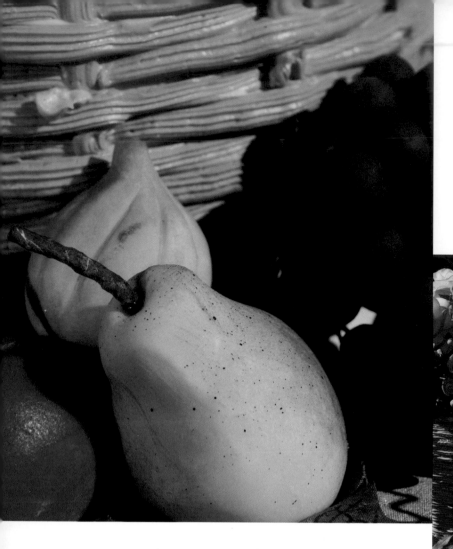

FOR YEARS, MAY AND JUNE WERE CONSIDERED THE BEST MONTHS FOR A NUPTIAL, BUT NO MORE: COUPLES LOVE ALL THE SEASONS. A WEDDING CAKE CAN ENHANCE AND ENCHANT WHETHER THE CEREMONY IS HELD IN THE WINTER, SPRING, SUMMER, OR FALL.

For a country club wedding, I decided to use a wicker basket effect for the sides of a multitiered cake. I would not recommend this look for a city ballroom event, but that doesn't mean it wasn't sophisticated, or in any way low key. Quite the opposite: We went all out to create the look of woven baskets done in buttercream with bushels of sugar flowers—tulips, calla lilies, roses, green hydrangeas, and branches of berries. Alongside the cake were marzipan fruit, and from far away the enormous cake had the look of a lush, rustic cornucopia. The size and color of this large cake attracted the guests to closely examine its woven basketweave effect and the decorations of sugar roses, pears, grapes, and acorns. Many found it hard to believe they'd be served a slice of this fantasy for dessert.

Brides today are fearless about color. No longer content with pretty pastels, they venture into elegant, tasteful tonalities—brown, beige, burnt orange, and olive—that reflect a boldness of choice. When a couple comes in to select colors for their cake, we often flip through a color wheel or stack of paint chips, so I can be sure the artists in my custom-shop will get the shade exactly right. The cake colors shown here are appropriate for birthdays, weddings, or for a groom's cake.

Anything is possible. This sugar crown, covered in edible gold leaf, was a fun project to conceive and a challenge to make. Opposite: Sugar dough bows and ribbons are part of our repertoire; a pastry crimper is used to make the seam marks in the ribbon.

Creepy Crawly Cake

IMPROVISE! THESE BLACK WIDOW
SPIDERS SIT ON A SUGARY WEB
AND ARE EASILY ASSEMBLED
WITH BLACK LICORICE LEGS FOR
A HALLOWEEN PARTY.

Ghosts, goblins, and goodies—that's what Halloween is all about. The trick of making it a night all ages enjoy is one that's easily solved by creating details to delight everyone, the way Carolyne Roehm did for this party. These chocolate-covered black widow spider cakes look scary enough to spook little children, who find a wicked delight in eating something that seems creepy. Adults, on the other hand, get a kick out of the ingenuity it takes to put together a cake that fits the ghoulish décor and tastes absolutely delicious. What's fun about these cakes is how easy they are to create with chocolate cake, frosting, and black licorice sticks. Forgo the sugary webs, if you're pressed for time—or have your children draw them on a piece of waxed paper as place settings for these artful arachnids.

This page: Guests received their own black widow spider cakes. Opposite: Boo-tiful, indeed! Glow-in-the-dark skulls greeted each guest at his or her place at the table, while silver jack-o'-lanterns decorated the buffet.

Isn't It Romantic?

WHAT AN EXCITING-LOOKING CAKE!
I LOVE IT WHEN A BRIDE SAYS,
"MRS. WEINSTOCK, I DON'T WANT IT SUBDUED!
THE MAN I'M MARRYING IS GREAT FUN AND
WE'RE GOING TO HAVE A GREAT LIFE TOGETHER!"
JUST THE COLORS SHOW YOU THAT THE BRIDE HAS SPIRIT.

MAKE ME THE MOST EXCITING CAKE YOU CAN WITHOUT FIREWORKS COMING OUT OF THE CENTER. THAT'S THE FEELING I GOT FROM THE BRIDE, WHO LOVED COLOR.

She also wanted all the wonderful flowers of the season. "I want the tulips. I want the peonies. I want the roses. I want the calla lilies . . ." The list went on and on. There was color on the cake as well: The motif that goes around each of the borders is almost Indian in feeling. This cake had to have a strong presence because the party was in a hotel ballroom, which was very "establishment" in its own way. They probably had close to 300 guests. You'll notice the chairs look comfortable and the centerpieces are very rich—and the way the room is set up, it's surprisingly intimate. It's a very romantic look— don't you think so? The candlelight is absolutely magical. Look at the room—who wouldn't want it?

One tradition I always suggest: The bride should take the top of the cake home to freeze, so she can share it with her husband on their first anniversary. The cake will last—and be a reminder of their happy day.

Left: Sometimes an initial sketch doesn't capture the spirit or nuance of what a bride wants but helps her give us more direction—to make it less stiff, or more young and stylish. Opposite: What a profusion of color! The pattern of the lace is beautiful, but it's the vivid flowers that make it really stand out.

Ready for a Close-Up

YOU MIGHT THINK BLACK AND WHITE
WOULDN'T WORK AS A COLOR SCHEME FOR
A WEDDING CAKE. BUT THINK AGAIN.

TRADITION USED TO DICTATE THAT THE COLOR BLACK WAS INAPPROPRIATE FOR A WEDDING. BUT MODERN TIMES CALL FOR A MODERN APPROACH, WHICH IS HOW THE DRAMATIC DESIGN FOR THIS CAKE CAME ABOUT.

Not every girl loves pink, and we all know by now that there are no rules saying you have to choose pastels for your bridesmaid dresses or the decoration on your wedding cake. When I'm creating a cake, I have to read the bride and decide: Should the cake be dainty with lace and bows in buttercream or should I employ what I call the 3Ds (dynamic, dramatic, and decadent details)? One of the most stunning brides I've ever seen was wearing a white gown with a thin black-and-white-striped ribbon around her waist—the simplicity of it was surprising. In the same way, black and white is an unexpected color combination for a cake, and when decorated with ruby red sugar flowers, the effect is dramatic. It's modern without being edgy or odd—there's a beauty and classicism to it that appeals to a discerning client.

Even in our studio, the color scheme of black, white, and red is eye-catching. Doesn't this cake just speak romance? When you set sugar bouquets of red tulips and full-blown roses against a graphic background, it makes a lasting impression.

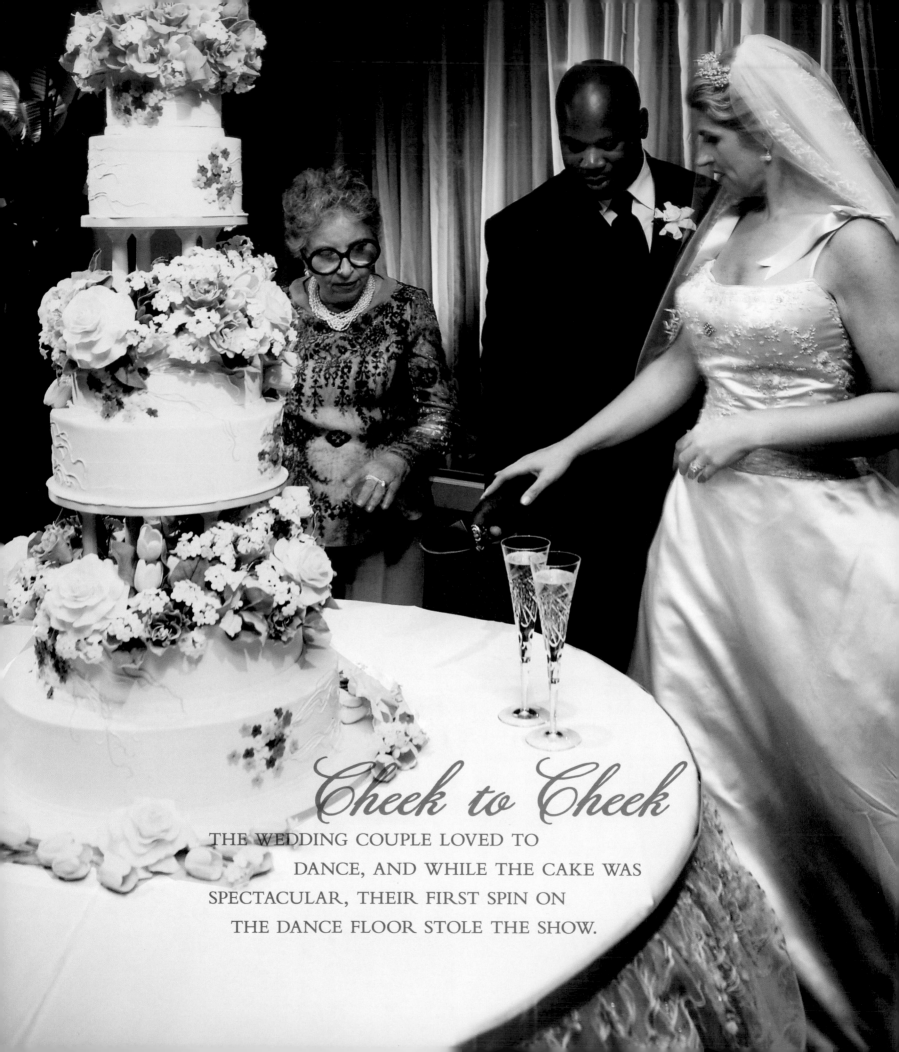

Cheek to Cheek

THE WEDDING COUPLE LOVED TO
DANCE, AND WHILE THE CAKE WAS
SPECTACULAR, THEIR FIRST SPIN ON
THE DANCE FLOOR STOLE THE SHOW.

"OPEN YOUR EYES: THIS IS A CELEBRATION OF YOUR LIFE." THAT'S WHAT I LIKE TO TELL THE BRIDE AND GROOM BEFORE THE BIG DAY. BUT THIS BEAUTIFUL COUPLE HAD ALREADY LEARNED THIS LESSON BY HEART.

Formal doesn't have to mean stuffy. You can bring so many elements into a wedding to make it special. I love meeting couples who know how to spread the joy around. This pair was lots of fun. She is in the wedding business; he is a fireman, and they had taken ballroom dancing together and built up quite a repertoire of moves. During the reception, they took to the floor and performed a dance that was extraordinary. I think Fred Astaire and Ginger Rogers should hand off the mantle to them!

The bride was also very smart about the pace of the party. During the cocktail hour, she put the wedding cake in a central spot where people would be drawn to it to ooh and ahh and chat up a storm. When it was time for guests to take their seats for dinner, the wedding couple and their parents stayed behind to cut the cake and take pictures. Sure, the bride wanted to show off the cake so everyone could enjoy the artistry of it, but she also wanted to forgo the time-consuming, after-dinner cake-cutting ritual so that the cake could be served as dessert. That left more time for the assembled to kick up their heels!

Sugar Baby Cakes

A WEDDING FAVOR IS A
LITTLE TREAT FOR GUESTS
TO THANK THEM FOR BEING
A PART OF A PERFECT DAY.

Everyone knows the saying, "It's the thought that counts." It is one of those phrases that's overused, but that is because it's really true. Especially when it comes to wedding favors, which couples now love to include as part of the ritual of getting married. Wedding favors are often commemorative—a matchbox with the couple's name and the date of the big day—or sweet—a small cake with a flower or simple motif that ties it into a detail on the wedding cake. I've produced many of these mini-cakes, so when I was asked to create a small favor with Godiva Chocolatier, I knew immediately what I wanted to design: a triple-tiered chocolate cake with stylized flowers, piping, or beadwork that symbolized our usual decorations. I liked the idea of these even more than the more extravagant mini-cakes: These favors appeal to my frugal nature, and the little boxes they come in are easy for guests to carry home.

We're known for the flowers on our wedding cakes, so it seemed fitting to have blossoms on the wedding favors I designed in chocolate. Milk chocolate cakes have dark chocolate ganache filling; the white chocolate ones are filled with hazelnut praline.

Colorful and Collectible

ANYTHING CAN BE THE INSPIRATION FOR
A CAKE. SO WHEN A COUPLE CAME IN WITH
A REQUEST FOR A CAKE INSPIRED BY A FAVORITE
COLLECTIBLE, WE LOVED THE CHALLENGE.

MAKING A CAKE INVOLVES ARTISTRY AND SKILL, BUT IT'S ABOUT TIMING, TOO. ONE OF THE BIGGEST CHALLENGES IS TO DO A CAKE THAT IS BEAUTIFUL AND ABSOLUTELY DELICIOUS. I SET OUT TO FIND A WAY TO BAKE, FILL, ICE, AND DECORATE A CAKE SO IT WILL BE AS SCRUMPTIOUS INSIDE AS IT IS ON THE OUTSIDE.

Starting out many years ago, I used to follow the rules. Cakes would come out fine, but when I altered the recipes, my experiments would backfire. Then I met a pastry chef who taught me how to change the formulas to suit my needs. One of my big issues was fondant.

Fondant is a commercially available sugar formula that many bakers use to ice cakes. Fondant sets up firm and hard when applied to a cake, very much like a clay coating. When iced with fondant, a cake cannot be refrigerated because the concentrated sugar in it attracts moisture. The chances are that a fondant-coated cake hasn't been refrigerated for a week or more. I hate fondant and never use it. Because a fondant-iced cake has to sit out, it changes the quality of the cake inside; you can't use whipped cream, and fresh fruits get moldy. There is no way that a cake like this one, made in stages, but assembled in one day, would look as fun and taste as delicious if I were using fondant.

Here's the story behind it. Many people collect the whimsical pottery and décor made by MacKenzie-Childs, and a couple celebrating their wedding anniversary wanted a cake that represented their passion for the collection. "Here's your challenge," the wife said. "We love this bench—please create a cake like it." She showed me a photo, and after I did a little of my own research, I found other inspiring pieces too, like a teapot. After all, you don't have to slavishly copy something—it's better, in fact, to improvise and make something surprising and new.

In the studio, Emily Roediger-Philpot, works her magic inspired by a floral design on a majolica teapot. These hand-decorated pieces are characterized by colorful stripes, checks, and patterns, all easily translated into sugar dough and painted with edible food coloring.

MY PHILOSOPHY IS THAT CAKE SHOULD BE ENJOYED BY ALL OF THE SENSES—IT SHOULD LOOK INTERESTING, SMELL DELICIOUS, AND TASTE HEAVENLY. YOU MAY WANT TO TOUCH IT—TO SEE IF IT'S REAL OR SUGAR—AND I ALWAYS HOPE TO HEAR PEOPLE SAY, "I CAN'T BELIEVE IT—COME AND LOOK!" WHEN THEY SEE ONE OF MY CAKES.

A tremendous amount of skill goes into a cake like this one, from painting on details and duplicating the side rails to building the wooden support structure and creating the sugar bouquet (yes, the pink gerberas and orange lilies are sugar!). The cake was around 40 inches long. Look closely at the printout of the MacKenzie-Childs piece that inspired this amazing confection: It's called the Ridiculous Bench!

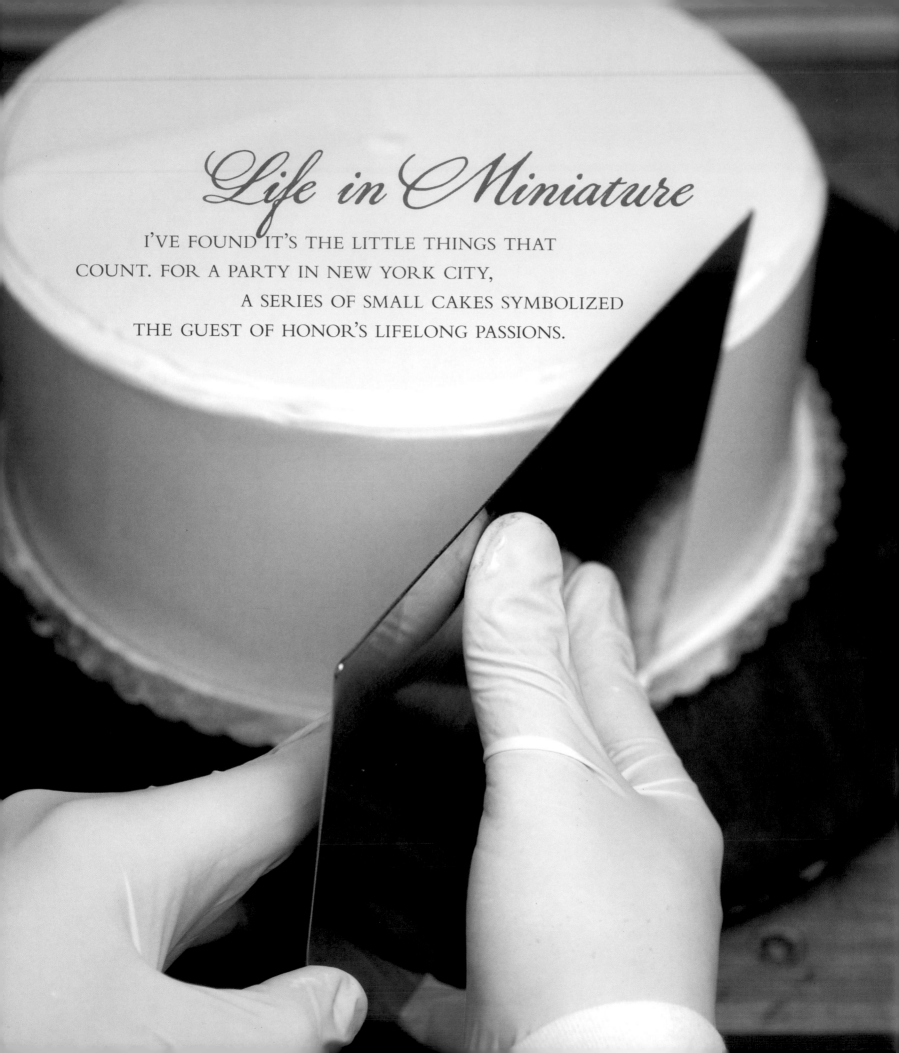

Life in Miniature

I'VE FOUND IT'S THE LITTLE THINGS THAT
COUNT. FOR A PARTY IN NEW YORK CITY,
A SERIES OF SMALL CAKES SYMBOLIZED
THE GUEST OF HONOR'S LIFELONG PASSIONS.

CELEBRATIONS
ARE WONDERFUL
MARKING POINTS IN
A LIFE CYCLE. I TELL
EVERYONE THAT IT'S
NOT JUST ABOUT
THE PARTY—IT'S
WHAT THE PARTY IS
ABOUT THAT'S
IMPORTANT—AND
THE CAKE WILL TELL
A DELICIOUS STORY.

Yellow cakes with vanilla crème filling were made for the party. Each one was a little stage for the icons from the guest of honor's life: memorable trips were commemorated by a camel and a gorilla; pink hydrangeas edged the cake topped by a pretty frock symbolizing his daughters. The invitation to the party was a printed tie, which we duplicated as well. The Empire State Building made an appearance, which I carefully put in place. His pet Yorkie and a steam train were also part of the birthday memorabilia.

Clowning Around

WHAT'S MORE FUN THAN A CLOWN AT A CHILD'S PARTY? THIS IS ONE OF THOSE CAKES THAT WILL MAKE EVERYONE SMILE.

Round cakes are made in a methodical way. Layers of cake are stacked one by one with the fillings between each layer. This stack of layers is then carved into a globe. After icing, the decorating begins. Brushes and colorful dusting powders are used to enhance the shades on the sugar dough. There's a little fairy dust applied too: The sparkle is a commercial product (dry gum Arabic) called edible glitter.

The first birthday cake I made was for a party in the backyard of our house on Long Island for my oldest daughter. I think it was a simple one—a strawberry shortcake with a single candle. Since then, I've done so many it's impossible to count them, but I can assure you of one thing—a clown cake will always get the biggest response at a children's birthday party. Boys and girls react with such glee when they see it! We used to do a round cake with a clown's face on it, but we started putting the clown on top of the cake—it's fun and appeals to the child in everyone.

This page: Sugar dough cards are hand-painted to look like the ones used in magic tricks. The cards sat on the side of the magician's hat decorated with colorful sprinkles of sugar confetti. Opposite: Every part of this figure is edible, but there are times when people can't bear to demolish the sweet artistry of these cakes.

Do You Believe in Magic?

A CAKE SHOULD BE A FANTASY THAT ENCHANTS EVERYONE. AT A BIRTHDAY PARTY FOR A YOUNG GIRL, AN ADORABLE PINK BUNNY DOES THE TRICK.

What's always important to me is to make a cake that's appropriate for the occasion. That's why I like to get to know something about the event—the theme or color of the décor—or a little something about the guest of honor. In this case, it was a birthday bash for a girl on the threshold of young womanhood. She was turning 13, and loved magic tricks and the color pink. I came up with a cake in the shape of a magician's hat with a pink sugar dough rabbit coming out of the top of it. I love the challenge of making animal cakes, and throughout the years we've made a Noah's Ark worth of creatures: a hippo, a giraffe, tigers, crocodiles, and monkeys, plus an armadillo for a party in Texas. We've had our fair share of birds, bugs, fish, and adorable dogs of all breeds. Not surprisingly, everyone loved this cute bunny, especially its long dark eyelashes and toothy grin, and I suspect that when the birthday girl gets older and memories of her big day start to fade, her magical pink bunny will remain clear in her mind.

Where's the Fire?

THE GROOM'S CAKE IS A TRADITION THAT
STARTED IN THE SOUTH, BUT THERE ARE NO
SET RULES WHEN IT COMES TO CREATING A
SENSATIONAL CAKE FOR THE MAN OF THE MOMENT.

Opposite: Traditionally, a groom's cake is chocolate or fruitcake, but I encourage everyone to make his or her own traditions and choose the flavor or theme that reflects the groom—like this fire truck done in miniature. This page: The couple rode a fire truck to the wedding ceremony. Here's a look at the real fire engine and fire station where the groom works.

Groom's cakes are popular nowadays in all parts of the country. What I like about these cakes is that they reflect the personality, interests, or hobbies of the groom. After all, in the excitement of the ceremony and the focus on the bride, he is often overlooked or even ignored! At this Nashville wedding, that was hardly the case. The handsome groom was a fireman, and his fire station honored him with a groom's cake—and it was clear immediately what would go on top. The artists in my studio made the perfect miniature fire truck for the otherwise unadorned white cake.

A groom's cake is often the dessert at a rehearsal dinner or can be served as an alternate dessert at the wedding. Traditionally it was sliced and boxed for single women attending the wedding to take home and put underneath their pillows. The idea was that the man they dreamed about would be their future husband. And what if they had a dreamless night? Well, in my mind they'd at least have something delicious to wake up to and eat.

Wine lore says a bacchanalia was a festival to honor Bacchus, the god of wine, and that women were the main revelers at these secret celebrations. But at a birthday party for a wine lover, everyone was happy to partake in these cakes made in the shape of wine bottles with customized labels. Marzipan grapes, sugar dough vines, and a faux wooden crate cake rounded out the effect. Cheers!

Fit for Royalty

FABERGÉ EGGS WERE THE
INSPIRATION FOR THIS EVENT, AND
EACH COLORFUL CAKE EVOKES THE
GILDED MINIATURES THAT FAMED JEWELER
PETER CARL FABERGÉ CREATED SO LONG AGO.

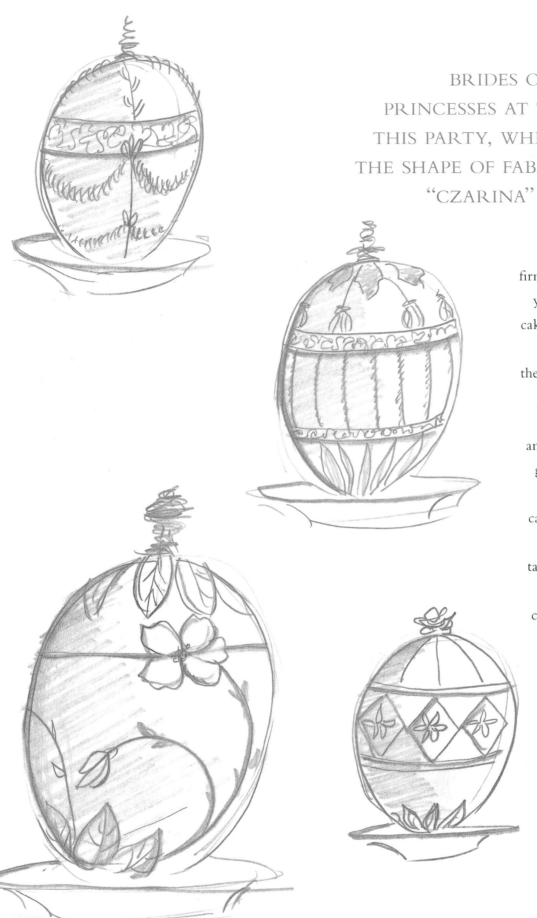

BRIDES OFTEN SAY THEY FEEL LIKE PRINCESSES AT THEIR WEDDINGS, BUT AT THIS PARTY, WHERE MINIATURE CAKES IN THE SHAPE OF FABERGÉ EGGS WERE SERVED, "CZARINA" WAS MORE APPROPRIATE.

I love it when couples come to me with a firm idea of what they want. For a party a few years ago, a couple asked that I create mini-cakes inspired by Fabergé eggs. It was easy for me to fall in love with that idea because of the history of these fabled enameled pieces. In 1885, a Russian czar ordered the very first one for his twentieth wedding anniversary, and his wife, the czarina, fell in love with his gift. How wonderful it was that many years later, in 2006, a couple wanted these mini-cakes for a postnuptial celebration in a loft in New York City! They liked a variety of tastes, too, combinations that you might love for your wedding cake: almond cake with caramel crème; espresso cake with chocolate mousse; white cake with raspberry crème; yellow lemon pound cake with key lime crème; yellow cake with blood orange crème; and carrot cake with coconut crème—all delicious! After all, as beautiful as these cakes were, they were meant to be eaten.

I did research about Fabergé eggs, but these cakes are not exact duplications. We did adaptations of some of the more famous ones, such as the lily of the valley Fabergé egg. Each had a special detail—some had silver or 24-karat gold leaf applied on buttercream—and the colors were divine.

"LIFE OF THE PARTY" IS A PHRASE THAT COULD APPLY TO OUR CAKES. THAT MAY SOUND LIKE AN IMMODEST THING TO SAY, BUT I DON'T MEAN TO BRAG. IF YOU LOOK AT THE ECLECTIC MIX OF CAKES ON THE FOLLOWING PAGES, YOU'LL SEE HOW EACH ONE CALLS FORTH A MOOD, LOOK, OR ATTITUDE THAT GETS PEOPLE TALKING. WHAT'S INSPIRING IS THAT YOU CAN CREATE ALMOST ANYTHING IN SUGAR DOUGH AND BUTTERCREAM!

A party owes its excitement to the energy that the host and hostess put into it—and our cakes reflect that excitement in colorful and varied ways. Each cake tells a story: We've made a French porcelain faience vase (one of my favorite cakes ever!); a true-to-life figurine; sunflowers and a silver dove; a shopping bag of gerbera daisies; the Empire State Building and the New York skyline. Another clever idea that we brought to life: a champagne bucket with sugar "ice" crystals. Almost any kind of creature works for the top of a festive cake, from a pink piggy and wise owl to a rubber ducky (who's that on its back?) for a baby's birthday.

PLANNING A PARTY TAKES A LITTLE IMAGINATION, A LOT OF WORK, AND THE ABILITY TO CREATE SOMETHING OUT OF THIN AIR. ONE OF THE MOST SATISFYING PARTS OF MY BUSINESS IS THAT I'M ALLOWED TO JOIN IN AND SHARE PEOPLE'S HAPPIEST MOMENTS, AND PARTICIPATE BY TREATING THEIR LOVED ONES TO THE MOST DELICIOUS, BEAUTIFUL, AND ORIGINAL CAKE THAT REPRESENTS THIS JOYOUS MOMENT.

Every princess has her castle—and why shouldn't it be created from sugar, spice, and everything nice? A powerful magazine editor decided to honor an international guest at a fête by ordering this sombrero cake for him. My "crooked" cake is a topsy-turvy stack of sweetness. I can't count the number of times I've handed the world over to a client. Welcome to the monkey house: I never tire of creating any species in sugar—and for this delightful cake, we made these cute monkeys. This is the kind of cake that makes people smile as soon as they see it. Oh, the games people play: I've made many a cake inspired by the love of chess, tennis, basketball, baseball, soccer, you name it! This backgammon board was a groom's cake.

EACH CAKE TELLS ITS OWN SPECIAL STORY. I LIKE TO DOCUMENT THE ONES WE MAKE BECAUSE THE PHOTOS REVEAL A KIND OF HISTORY OF THE PEOPLE, IMAGES, AND THEMES THAT PEOPLE ADORE. I ALSO FIND THAT THIS SCRAPBOOK OF MOMENTS REMINDS ME OF THE FUN WE HAD FIGURING OUT HOW TO MAKE EACH DREAM BECOME REAL IN SUGAR.

During the holidays at the end of the year, our staff takes a break. But most of the time, we're designing, baking, making, icing, decorating, and shipping our beautiful cakes almost every day of the week so people will have them for their evening, weekend, and special-occasion parties. Guests of honor delight in valise cakes with international stickers, and we've made innumerable taxis, hot rods, convertibles, and Rolls-Royces, not to mention decorating hundreds of vases of sugar gladiolus, roses, poppies, and hydrangea by hand. Figurines are always a challenge, whether someone wants a merry jack-in-the-box, Marilyn Monroe, or an amphibious bride and groom.

The Art
of Making
a Cake

Classic Yellow Cake

Everyone loves this buttery cake—and we've perfected this one over time so it's the only yellow cake recipe you'll ever want to bake.

2¼	cups sifted cake flour
2	teaspoons baking powder
½	teaspoon salt
½	teaspoon ginger
½	pound (2 sticks) unsalted butter, at room temperature
2	cups sugar
4	large egg yolks
1	cup milk
2	teaspoons vanilla extract
1	cup sour cream
4	large egg whites

1. Preheat the oven to 350 degrees. Butter two 8 x 3-inch round baking pans or one 12 x 3-inch round or square pan and line them with parchment.

2. Sift together the flour, baking powder, salt, and ginger. Set aside.

3. In a large bowl of an electric mixer, cream the butter until fluffy and light in color, about 2 minutes on medium speed. Add the sugar and continue to mix until fluffy and light.

4. Add the egg yolks, one at a time, being sure each is blended before adding the next. Add the milk and vanilla.

5. Reduce the mixer speed to low and add the flour mixture alternately with the sour cream, beginning and ending with the flour. Be sure the mixture is completely blended after each addition. Scrape the sides of the bowl, and beat for 1 minute.

6. In a separate bowl, using a clean whisk attachment, beat the egg whites on high speed until soft peaks form.

7. Gently fold the whipped egg whites into the batter with a rubber spatula.

8. Pour the batter into the prepared pans and smooth with a rubber spatula. Place the pans in the center of the oven and bake for 45 to 50 minutes until the sides of the cake pull away from the pan and a toothpick inserted in the center comes out clean. The top of the cake should be nicely browned.

Serves 12—15

SUGGESTED WASH FLAVORS: Raspberry, strawberry, lemon, orange

SUGGESTED FILLINGS: Raspberry or strawberry buttercream, lemon or orange buttercream, mocha buttercream, chocolate mousse

Chocolate Fudge Cake

A hint on making this fudge cake a hit: Make sure the cocoa powder mixture is at room temperature before you add it to the rest of the recipe.

⅔   cup water
¾   cup unsweetened cocoa powder
2   tablespoons vanilla extract
¼   cup brewed coffee
1   pound (4 sticks) unsalted butter, at room temperature
2⅓   cups sugar
12   large eggs
11½   ounces unsweetened chocolate, melted
2½   cups cake flour
1   tablespoon baking soda

1. Preheat the oven to 300 degrees. Butter two 8 x 3-inch baking pans or one 12 x 3-inch round or square pan and line them with parchment.

2. In a small saucepan, bring the water to a boil. Pour the boiling water into a bowl and add the cocoa powder, vanilla, and coffee, whisking vigorously until the mixture is smooth and no lumps remain. Set aside and let the mixture cool to room temperature.

3. In a large bowl of an electric mixer, cream the butter on medium speed for 3 minutes. Add the sugar and mix for another 3 minutes, or until the batter is light in color and fluffy. Add the eggs, one at a time. Stop the mixer and scrape down the sides with a rubber spatula.

4. Add the melted chocolate and mix on medium speed for 1 minute, until all the chocolate is well incorporated.

5. Sift the flour and baking soda together. Reduce the mixer speed to low, and add the flour mixture alternately with the cocoa mixture, beginning and ending with the flour.

6. Pour the batter into the prepared pans and place the pans in the center of the oven. Bake for 60 to 70 minutes until the sides of the cake pull away from the pan and a toothpick inserted in the center comes out clean. This cake is dense and bakes more evenly in a slow oven

Serves 12—15

SUGGESTED WASH FLAVORS: Raspberry, strawberry, orange, hazelnut, coffee

SUGGESTED FILLINGS: Raspberry or strawberry buttercream, orange buttercream, basic buttercream, mocha buttercream, chocolate mousse

NOTE: For a richer tasting cake, you can substitute coffee for the ⅔ cup water.

How to Cut Cake Layers

There are a few essential tools that help you to trim, slice, and fill a cake. These include a turntable; various-sized cake cardboards; a long, sharp, serrated knife; and a long icing spatula.

Opposite: Cakes usually mound up on top, and one of my staff, Julie Yurigma Campuzano, demonstrates how to slice off and trim the cake to get a flat-top that's easy to slice into discs and fill.

1. Cakes usually have a slight mound on top, which must be sliced off to get a flat-topped cake that can then be sliced into one-half inch to one-inch thick layers. (See page 197 to see an example of trimming.)

2. Place the cooled cake on a cardboard cake board and set on the turntable. Using a long, serrated knife, mark the cake horizontally in one-half inch to one-inch thick intervals. A cake baked in an 8 X 3-inch pan will usually yield two or three layers, depending on which cake you have used—some bake higher than others. Hold the knife against the cake and parallel to the base of the turntable, and turn the turntable while keeping the knife at arm level. Apply a subtle, but firm inward pressure, allowing the knife to go deeper to cut through the cake; this is the first slice.

3. Take a long icing spatula and lift the edge of the cake slice slightly. Slide a cardboard cake base under the first top layer, and remove. Repeat until you have sliced the whole cake. It is important that the cake slices be completely cooled before you fill them; otherwise, the filling will soften, melt, and make a mess.

Hazelnut Cake

You'll need to put a bit more effort into this cake, but it's well worth it. Grind the hazelnuts into a powder with a food processor, but don't overdo it or you'll be left with hazelnut butter.

10	large egg yolks
1¾	cups sugar
5	teaspoons vanilla extract
2½	tablespoons almond extract
⅓	cup sifted cake flour
⅓	cup unsweetened cocoa powder
8	cups whole skinned hazelnuts, ground to make 4 cups hazelnut flour
10	large egg whites

1. Preheat the oven to 350 degrees. Butter two 8 x 3-inch baking pans or one 12 x 3-inch round or square pan and line them with parchment.

2. In a large bowl of an electric mixer, beat the egg yolks until pale yellow ribbons form when the beaters are lifted. Add 1¼ cups of the sugar and the vanilla and almond extracts and beat on high speed until light and airy. Set aside.

3. Combine the cake flour, cocoa powder, and hazelnut flour and mix with a rubber spatula. Using the rubber spatula, fold one-third of the flour mixture into the yolk mixture, folding gently until just incorporated. Repeat with the remaining flour mixture, adding one-third at a time.

4. In another large mixing bowl, using a clean whisk attachment, beat the egg whites on medium speed. Just as they start to get foamy, add the remaining ½ cup sugar in a slow stream. Beat the whites until stiff peaks form. When the beaters are removed, you should have peaks that stand straight up.

5. With a rubber spatula, gently fold about 2 cups of the egg whites into the flour mixture, just enough to lighten the batter. Working quickly, fold in the remainder of the whites.

6. Pour the mixture into the prepared pans and place the pans in the center of the oven. Bake for 40 minutes until the sides of the cake pull away from the pan and a toothpick inserted in the center comes out clean. The cake will be springy to the touch and brown on top.

Serves 12—15

SUGGESTED WASH FLAVORS: Orange, hazelnut

SUGGESTED FILLINGS: Mocha buttercream, chocolate mousse

Lady Baltimore White Cake

The name of this confection may have originated in the South, but it's a beautiful, delicious cake that's enjoyed everywhere.

¾   cup (1½ sticks) unsalted butter at room temperature
2   cups sugar
3   cups sifted cake flour
3   teaspoons baking powder
½   teaspoon salt
½   cup water
½   cup milk
1   teaspoon vanilla extract
6   large egg whites

1. Preheat the oven to 350 degrees. Butter two 8 x 3-inch baking pans or one 12 x 3-inch round or square pan and line them with parchment.

2. In a large bowl of an electric mixer, cream the butter and sugar at medium speed until light and fluffy, about 2 minutes.

3. Sift the flour, baking powder, and salt together; set aside.

4. Combine the water, milk, and vanilla. Add to the sugar and butter mixture alternately with the flour mixture, beating until smooth after each addition.

5. In a separate bowl, using a clean whisk attachment, beat the egg whites on high speed until soft peaks form.

6. Gently fold the whipped egg whites into the batter using a rubber spatula. Stop as soon as the whites are well incorporated.

7. Pour the batter into the prepared pans and place the pans in the center of the oven. Bake for 30 to 40 minutes until the sides of the cake pull away from the pan and a toothpick inserted in the center comes out clean. The cake should be nicely browned on top.

Serves 12—15

SUGGESTED WASH FLAVORS: Orange, lemon, raspberry, strawberry, hazelnut

SUGGESTED FILLINGS: Orange buttercream, raspberry or strawberry buttercream, mocha buttercream, chocolate mousse

Spice Cake

A surprising number of brides order spice cake as an alternative to the classic yellow or white cake for a wedding, but this light, tasty recipe works well for any occasion.

2½   cups sifted cake flour
1½   teaspoons unsweetened cocoa powder
1   teaspoon baking powder
¼   teaspoon baking soda
1   teaspoon ground cinnamon
½   teaspoon ground cloves
½   teaspoon ground allspice
3   large eggs
1   cup milk
¼   pound (1 stick) unsalted butter at room temperature
2   cups sugar

1. Preheat the oven to 325 degrees. Butter two 8 x 3-inch baking pans or one 12 x 3-inch round or square pan and line them with parchment.

2. In a large mixing bowl, sift the flour, cocoa powder, baking powder, baking soda, and spices. In a small bowl, combine the eggs and milk.

3. In a bowl of an electric mixer, cream the butter and sugar at medium speed until light and fluffy, about 2 minutes.

4. Add one-third of the flour mixture to the butter mixture, then one-third of the egg mixture, and mix on low speed until completely blended. Continue adding the flour and egg mixtures alternately, mixing until the batter is smooth and lump-free.

5. Pour the batter into the prepared pans and place the pans in the center of the oven. Bake for 40 to 50 minutes until the sides of the cake pull away from the pan and a toothpick inserted in the center comes out clean.

Serves 12—15

SUGGESTED WASH FLAVORS: Raspberry, strawberry, orange, apricot

SUGGESTED FILLINGS: Raspberry or strawberry buttercream, orange buttercream, mocha buttercream, chocolate mousse

Almond Cake

You can make almond flour by grinding skinned almonds in a food processor, but make sure to monitor it and stop processing when the nuts are ground to a fine flour texture.

10	large egg yolks
1¾	cups sugar
5	teaspoons vanilla extract
2½	tablespoons almond extract
5	cups slivered almonds, ground to make 4 cups almond flour
⅓	cup sifted cake flour
10	large egg whites

1. Preheat the oven to 350 degrees. Butter two 8 x 3-inch baking pans or one 12 x 3-inch round or square pan and line them with parchment.

2. In a large bowl of an electric mixer, combine the egg yolks, 1¼ cups of the sugar, and the vanilla and almond extracts. Mix on medium speed until pale yellow ribbons form when the beaters are lifted, about 10 minutes.

3. Fold the almond flour into the cake flour with a rubber spatula. Reduce the mixer speed to low and add one-third of the flour mixture to the yolk mixture. Add the next third and incorporate well, then add the rest.

4. In another mixer bowl, using a clean whisk attachment, beat the egg whites on high speed until they begin to foam. Add the remaining ½ cup sugar and continue to beat until soft peaks form.

5. Using a large rubber spatula, fold a quarter of the whipped egg whites into the yolk mixture. Gently fold in with the spatula, then add the rest of the whites and fold in. Stop as soon as the whites are incorporated.

6. Pour the batter into the prepared pans and place the pans in the center of the oven. Bake for about 30 minutes until the cake is nicely browned on top and a toothpick inserted in the center comes out clean. As this cake cools, it will shrink in the pans.

Serves 12—15

SUGGESTED WASH FLAVORS: Orange, hazelnut

SUGGESTED FILLINGS: Mocha buttercream, chocolate mousse

Carrot Cake

Marry this scrumptious cake with its proper mate—a cream cheese buttercream filling. I sometimes add raisins, dried cranberries, or dried cherries to the batter; pistachios and walnuts are also delightful additions.

2¼	cups sugar
4⅔	cups sifted cake flour
1½	teaspoons baking powder
1½	teaspoons baking soda
½	teaspoon salt
2	teaspoons ground cinnamon
1	teaspoon ground ginger
⅛	teaspoon ground allspice
1¾	cups vegetable oil
6	large eggs
3	cups grated carrots (about 10 medium carrots)

1. Preheat the oven to 350 degrees. Butter two 8 x 3-inch baking pans or one 12 x 3-inch round or square pan and line them with parchment.

2. In a bowl of an electric mixer, combine the sugar, flour, baking powder, baking soda, salt, and spices. Set on low speed and slowly pour the oil into the flour mixture. After all the oil is added and fully blended, add the eggs, one at a time. When the eggs are fully blended, add the carrots and continue to blend just until they are evenly mixed into the batter. Stop the mixer and scrape down the sides with a rubber spatula, then continue to beat on low for another 30 seconds.

3. Pour the batter into the prepared pans and place the pans in the center of the oven. Bake for 40 to 50 minutes until the sides of the cake pull away from the pan and a toothpick inserted in the center comes out clean.

Serves 12—15

SUGGESTED WASH FLAVORS: Orange, hazelnut, coffee

SUGGESTED FILLINGS: Orange cream cheese buttercream, cream cheese buttercream

Basic Buttercream Icing

Here are a few tricks of the trade. Be sure to use a clear vanilla if you want a pure white icing or you'll end up with more of an ivory icing with a bit of yellow tint. Use vegetable paste colors rather than food coloring to create different icing colors.

3½ cups sugar
¼ cup water
13 large egg whites
3 pounds (12 sticks) unsalted butter, at room temperature, cut into half sticks
6 tablespoons clear vanilla extract

1. In a medium saucepan, combine the sugar and water, mixing with a wooden spoon until the sugar is mostly dissolved. Place the pan on the stove and use a clean pastry brush to paint the area just above the water line with fresh water. Turn the heat to medium and watch the sugar mixture to be sure it doesn't caramelize or burn. Put a candy thermometer in the pan and simmer the sugar-water mixture without stirring until the thermometer reads 240 degrees (soft-ball stage); this will take 5 to 7 minutes.

2. Meanwhile, place the egg whites in a large bowl of an electric mixer. Using the whisk attachment, beat the egg whites at medium speed until they turn from opaque to white and begin to form soft peaks. They should be at least double in volume in 3 to 5 minutes. Do not overbeat, as this will cause the egg whites to lose their sheen and become dry.

3. When the sugar mixture reaches 240 degrees, turn the mixer on high speed and very carefully and slowly pour the hot sugar mixture in a very thin stream down the inside of the bowl (near the edge) and into the beaten egg whites. (Do not pour the hot syrup all at once directly into the middle of the eggs.) Beat for 20 to 35 minutes on medium to high speed. The egg whites will lose some of their volume and the mixture should resemble a very thick meringue. The outside of the bowl should be moderately warm to the touch.

4. At this point, reduce the speed to medium or low and add the butter pieces, one at a time. The mixture will break up and begin to look like cottage cheese, but don't worry. Keep the mixer running, continue adding butter, and let the mixer whip the buttercream until it begins to get smooth again; this could take up to 10 minutes. Once the mixture is smooth, add the vanilla and beat for 5 minutes more. The buttercream is now ready to be colored or chilled. (If the buttercream is too soft, chill for 10 minutes, then whip again. If this doesn't work, cream 4 tablespoons chilled butter, then gently whip the creamed butter into the buttercream, 1 tablespoon at a time. Beat until the buttercream is smooth and there are no lumps.)

NOTE ABOUT THE SUGAR AND WATER: This mixture should be at the soft-ball stage—240 degrees—when it goes into the egg whites. This means you must start to whip the egg whites before the sugar reaches the soft-ball stage. If you're not sure or have trouble reading the thermometer, remove a teaspoon of the sugar mixture with a metal spoon and drop it into a measuring cup of cold water. Using your fingers, reach into the water and try to gather up the mixture; you should be able to form a soft ball with it.

You can freeze extra buttercream icing for up to 3 months.
Makes 12 cups, enough to fill and ice two 4-layer 8-inch cakes or one 4-layer 12-inch cake

Chocolate Buttercream Icing

½   cup strong brewed coffee
¾   cup unsweetened cocoa powder
5   cups Basic Buttercream Icing
     (page 202)

1. Pour the coffee and cocoa powder into a medium mixing bowl and stir or whisk together until there are no lumps.

2. Blend 1 cup of the buttercream into the cocoa mixture and whisk or stir to combine, then add the cocoa mixture to the remaining buttercream and blend thoroughly until no streaks remain.

Makes 6 cups, enough to fill and ice one 4-layer 8-inch cake or one 4-layer 12-inch cake

Basic Buttercream Filling

The trick to perfecting buttercream filling is to carefully follow Step 3. Pour the hot liquid in a very thin stream down the side of the bowl or near the edge to avoid getting a scrambled-egg effect. If this happens, you have to throw out the filling and start again.

1   large egg
5   large egg yolks
2   cups sugar
⅓   cup water
1½ pounds (6 sticks) unsalted butter, at
     room temperature, cut into half
     sticks
6   tablespoons vanilla extract,
     or ⅓ to ½ cup flavored liqueur of
     choice

1. In a large bowl of an electric mixer, place the egg and yolks. Using the whisk attachment, beat at medium speed until the mixture turns from orange-yellow to pale yellow. Continue whisking while you proceed with Step 2.

2. In a medium saucepan, combine the sugar and water, mixing with a wooden spoon until the sugar is mostly dissolved. Place the pan on the stove and use a clean pastry brush to paint the area just above the water line with fresh water. Turn the heat to medium and watch the sugar mixture to be sure it doesn't caramelize or burn. Put a candy thermometer in the pan and simmer the sugar-water mixture without stirring until the thermometer reads 240 degrees (soft-ball stage); this will take 5 to 7 minutes.

3. With the mixer still running on medium speed, very carefully and slowly pour the hot sugar mixture in a very thin stream down the inside of the bowl (near the edge) and into the yolks. (Do not pour the hot syrup all at once directly into the middle of the eggs.) Beat for 12 to 15 minutes on medium speed, or until the outside of the bowl is moderately warm to the touch.

4. Add the butter pieces, one at a time. The mixture may break up and begin to look like cottage cheese, but don't worry. Keep the mixer running, continue adding butter, and let the mixer whip the buttercream until it begins to get smooth again; this could take up to 10 minutes. Once the mixture is smooth, add the vanilla or other flavoring and beat for 3 minutes more. (If the filling is too soft, chill for 10 minutes before you fill your cake. If this doesn't work, cream 4 tablespoons chilled butter, then gently whip the creamed butter into the filling, 1 tablespoon at a time.) The filling may be stored in an airtight container in the refrigerator for up to 5 days.

Makes 5 to 7 cups, enough to fill two 4-layer 8-inch cakes or one 4-layer 12-inch cake

Flavored Buttercream Fillings

Add the flavorings at the end when you add the butter.

RASPBERRY OR STRAWBERRY

5   cups Basic Buttercream Filling (page 204)
2   cups frozen raspberries or strawberries
¼   cup raspberry-flavored syrup, framboise liqueur, or strawberry-flavored syrup

Defrost the berries so that they are loose. Squeeze out as much excess liquid as possible and add the pulp to the buttercream filling. Add the syrup or liqueur and mix well. It's all right if the buttercream is lumpy.

Makes 6 cups, enough to fill two 4-layer 8-inch cakes or one 4-layer 12-inch cake

MOCHA

5   cups Basic Buttercream Filling (page 204)
2   ounces bittersweet chocolate, melted and cooled to room temperature
1½ tablespoons instant espresso powder
2   tablespoons coffee liqueur

In a large bowl of an electric mixer, blend ½ cup of the buttercream filling into the melted chocolate on medium-low speed. Stir in the espresso powder, then add the mixture to the remaining buttercream filling. Blend in the liqueur and mix for 1 minute.

Makes 6 cups, enough to fill two 4-layer 8-inch cakes or one 4-layer 12-inch cake

CHOCOLATE

½   cup strong brewed coffee
¾   unsweetened cocoa powder
¼   cup Grand Marnier, dark rum, or raspberry or hazelnut liqueur (optional)
5   cups Basic Buttercream Filling (page 204) or Basic Buttercream Icing (page 202)

NOTE: *Using Basic Buttercream Filling will yield a richer, slightly thicker filling, because there are egg yolks in the recipe; Basic Buttercream Icing, made with egg whites, results in a creamier filling.*

1. Pour the coffee and cocoa powder into a medium mixing bowl and stir or whisk together until there are no lumps. Add the flavoring, if using, and whisk until the mixture is well blended.

2. Stir 1 cup of the buttercream filling into the cocoa mixture and whisk or stir to blend, then add the cocoa mixture to the remaining buttercream filling and blend until thoroughly mixed and no streaks remain.

Makes 6 cups, enough to fill two 4-layer 8-inch cakes or one 4-layer 12-inch cake

CREAM CHEESE

2   cups (1 pound) cream cheese, at room temperature
6   cups Basic Buttercream Filling (page 204), at room temperature

In a bowl of an electric mixer, combine the cream cheese and buttercream filling and beat for 3 minutes on medium speed, or until no lumps remain.

Makes 6 cups, enough to fill two 4-layer 8-inch cakes or one 4-layer 12-inch cake

ORANGE

2-3 tablespoons freshly grated orange zest (from about 1 large or 2 small oranges)
1   tablespoon freshly grated lemon zest (from 1 lemon)
5   cups Basic Buttercream Filling (page 204)
2   tablespoons orange-flavored liqueur

1. In a large bowl of an electric mixer, mix 2 tablespoons of the orange zest and the lemon zest with the buttercream filling.

2. Blend in the liqueur. For stronger flavor, add 1 more tablespoon of orange zest after the liqueur has been added.

Makes 6 cups, enough to fill two 4-layer 8-inch cakes or one 4-layer 12-inch cake

LEMON

4   tablespoons freshly grated lemon zest (from 2 to 3 lemons)
5   cups Basic Buttercream Filling (page 204)
2   tablespoons orange-flavored liqueur
    Juice of 3 lemons

1. In a large bowl of an electric mixer, mix the lemon zest with the buttercream filling.

2. Blend the liqueur and lemon juice into 1 cup of the buttercream filling, then add to the remaining filling. Whip briefly on medium-low speed to combine.

Makes 6 cups, enough to fill two 4-layer 8-inch cakes or one 4-layer 12-inch cake

Chocolate Mousse Filling

This mousse is good enough to eat on its own. Be warned: Your family may never let you make any other kind of filling again.

1 pound semisweet or bittersweet chocolate
¼ pound (1 stick) unsalted butter
4 cups heavy cream
2 tablespoons powdered gelatin
7 large egg yolks
3 large egg whites
¼ cup sugar

1. Melt the chocolate and butter together in a double boiler set over gently simmering water. When the mixture has melted, remove it and set aside to cool to room temperature.

2. In a bowl of an electric mixer, pour 3 cups of the cream. With the whisk attachment, whip the cream to soft peaks, but do not overwhip. Refrigerate the whipped cream, covered. Dissolve the gelatin in water according to the package directions.

3. Pour the remaining 1 cup heavy cream into a small saucepan and bring to a simmer over low heat.

4. In a separate bowl, whisk the egg yolks together. Use a measuring cup to dip out ¼ cup of the hot cream, and pour it slowly into the yolks, whisking rapidly. Now pour the yolk mixture in a thin stream into the remaining cream, whisking rapidly as you pour. Pour in the dissolved gelatin, keeping the heat at low, and whisk constantly until the mixture begins to thicken, about 2 minutes. Do not let it simmer or boil. Remove from the heat, set the pan on top of a bowl of ice, and continue to whisk until the mixture is cool and thick.

5. Pour the mixture into the cooled chocolate and stir until incorporated. (If the chocolate breaks up, or gets grainy, beat with an electric or immersion blender, and add 3 tablespoons cold heavy cream.) Beat for 2 minutes, or until the mixture is silky and shiny.

6. In a large bowl of the mixer, using a clean whisk attachment, whip the egg whites and sugar together until stiff peaks form. Working quickly, fold in the chocolate mixture. Fold in the chilled whipped cream. Refrigerate for at least 3 hours before using.

Makes 8 cups, enough to fill two 4-layer 8-inch cakes or one 4-layer 12-inch cake

Washes: Simple Syrup

You can certainly skip this step to a perfect cake, but I thought I'd share my secret for those perfectionists out there. After the cake layers are baked and trimmed, I add flavor by brushing all of the layers with a wash before applying the filling. (I use a pastry brush or spray it on with a small plastic spray pump bottle.)

1 cup sugar
1 cup water

1. In a medium saucepan, combine the sugar and water. Bring to a boil over medium heat, and remove from the heat as soon as the sugar is dissolved.

2. Add ¼ cup of one or more of the following to make a flavored wash:

Hazelnut liqueur
Chocolate liqueur
Coffee liqueur
Raspberry liqueur
Orange liqueur
Vanilla extract
Almond extract
Lemon juice
Brewed coffee

Makes 1 cup, enough for one 4-layer 8-inch cake or one 4-layer 12-inch cake

Tip: Don't over-soak your cake layers, and there's no need to use expensive liqueur like Grand Marnier—after a fancy meal, that kind of extravagance is overkill! And if you have any simple syrup left over, drink it!

Photography Credits

These are the treasured hands of Vilna Peters, my assistant for 25 years.

Sylvie Becquet, pages 42, 43, 66, 67, 84, 85, 122, 123, 144, 145
Melanie Dunea, page 9
Terry deRoy Gruber, pages 34, 35, 36. 37
John Labbe, pages 1, 2, 3, 4, 5, 11, 12, 15, 17, 18. 19, 20, 22, 23, 24, 25, 26, 27, 28, 29, 30, 31, 32, 33, 48, 49, 50, 51, 52, 54, 55, 60, 61, 68, 69, 70, 71, 72, 73, 74, 75, 76, 77, 79, 80, 81, 82, 83, 86, 87, 88, 89, 91, 92, 95, 96, 97, 98, 99, 100, 101, 103, 104, 105, 106, 110, 111, 112, 113, 114, 115, 116, 117, 118, 119, 120, 124, 125, 126, 127, 128, 129, 130, 131, 132, 133, 134, 135, 136, 137, 138, 139, 140, 141, 142, 143, 150, 151, 153, 160, 161, 162, 163, 164, 165, 166, 167, 168, 169, 170, 171, 172, 173, 174, 175, 176, 177, 178, 179, 182, 183, 184, 187, 194, 197, 201, 202, 207, 208
Patricia Lyons, pages 38, 39, 40, 41, 62, 63, 64, 65
Sarah Marins, pages 146, 147, 149
Eadaoin Morrish, pages 44, 45, 46, 47
Corina Raznikov, pages 56, 57, 58, 59
Angela Talley, pages 107, 108, 109, 154, 155, 156, 157, 158, 159, 180, 181
Ben Weinstock, pages 188, 189, 190, 191, 192, 193

Published in 2008 by Stewart, Tabori & Chang
An imprint of Harry N. Abrams, Inc.

Text copyright © 2008 by Sylvia Weinstock

Library of Congress Cataloging-in-Publication Data

Weinstock, Sylvia.
Sylvia Weinstock's sensational cakes / Sylvia Weinstock ; book design by Doug Turshen with David Huang.
p. cm.
ISBN 978-1-58479-718-0
1. Desserts. 2. Cookery, American. I. Title.
TX773.W445 2008
641.8'6--dc22
2008008500

Editor: Jennifer Levesque
Designer: Doug Turshen with David Huang
Production Manager: Jacquie Poirier

The text of this book was composed in *Bembo, ITC Franklin Gothic,* and *Lili Wang*

Printed and bound in China
10 9 8 7 6 5 4 3 2 1

HNA
harry n. abrams, inc.
a subsidiary of La Martinière Groupe

115 West 18th Street
New York, NY 10011
www.hnabooks.com